CW00927228

IN THE LONG RUN

The Author, Minister of State at the Home Office, 1984-6.

In The Long Run
Tales of a Yorkshire Life

by

SIR GILES SHAW

The Memoir Club

© Giles Shaw 2001

First published in 2001 by
The Memoir Club
Whitworth Hall
Spennymoor
County Durham

British Library Cataloguing in
Publication Data.
A catalogue record for this book
is available from the
British Library.

ISBN: 1 84104 038 X

Typeset by George Wishart & Associates, Whitley Bay.
Printed by Bookcraft (Bath) Ltd.

For my family

Contents

List of Illustrations

Foreword
by Tam Dalyell MP

Giles Shaw was widely perceived as an asset to the House of Commons when he arrived, and a significant loss when he stood down. Why? Because he brought increasingly rare commodities to Parliament. A working knowledge of industry at middle/senior management level. An identification with the men and women of Yorkshire who sent him to Westminster, in an age when service to Party, or national reputation in the metropolis provided an easier passage. Unaffectatious humanity. And real, unwounding wit. It was not only his own colleagues in the Conservative Party, and some of his undergraduate friends who themselves had arrived in the House of Commons who liked and respected him. I assert as an MP intimately involved in the election of a Speaker, when Jack Weatherill donned his wig for the last time, that Giles would have received more Labour votes than either Peter Brooke, Margaret Thatcher's choice, or the very able Terence Higgins. That this was never put to the test, when Betty Boothroyd was chosen, was partly due to the prevailing spirit of the time, that the Speakership should go turn and turn about by Party, and partly due to the flaws in the way in which the Speaker is chosen when there are more than two candidates. The charm and fairness with which Giles operated as a senior member of the Speaker's Panel gave an appetising foretaste of the qualities which he would have brought to the Chair of the House of Commons, and which he brought three and a half decades before to the Presidency of the Cambridge Union. He is one of the most favourably and best-remembered undergraduates of the first half of the 1950s. For half a century I have heard variations of that 'sparkling, diminutive Giles Shaw'. Nor was he simply a 'union man'. The huge college of St Johns gave him their annual accolade as the undergraduate who contributed most to the college.

Everywhere he went, Giles was a life-enhancer with those whom he came into contact. After his moving funeral, the Headmaster of Sedbergh School told me of the wise service over years, which he had rendered to his school, finally as Chairman of the Board of Governors. As a cavalryman, in another regiment, I know of his fellow officers' and senior sergeants' view that Second Lieutenant Shaw was one of the best National Service subalterns that they ever had.

Not only the Royal Society for the Protection of Birds, but many others in the Environment movement knew him, as an ally with a unique first-hand knowledge. The well-being of Yorkshire people, particularly his constituents, many of whom developed a deep affection for him, and the countryside, its flora, fauna and birds were as important, if not more important to him than politics. And this is perhaps why the present volume, lovingly put together by Dione, whom his friends knew Giles simply adored, and the Spennymoor Memoir Club, is a memoir, and not a normal, commercially promoted biography.

Why did Giles, with all his talent, not achieve Cabinet rank? Contrary to what he says about turning down the Barnsley candidature, the advice from the Rowntree Chairman was bad. No way would a Conservative represent Barnsley. But had Rowntrees given him three weeks, he would have been an established Conservative candidate, and he, not Jonathan Aitken, would have been selected for Thirsk and Malton. Having fought a 'hopeless' seat is a huge advantage in a selection conference. Since the Labour candidate was my friend, Joan Maynard, 'Stalin's Grandmother', representative of the agricultural workers, calling for the nationalisation of all agricultural land, Giles would have walked the election in those broad acres. Had he entered the Commons at that time, he would have surely become a substantial figure much earlier.

As a member of Madame Speaker's Chairman's Panel, Giles enhanced the respect and affection of both those who shared, and did not share, his political opinions. At more than one critical moment, Betty Boothroyd sought his wise counsel, which he generously gave. No wonder. Giles encapsulated a civilised approach to life, which took into account the feelings of others.

Preface

THIS IS A YORKSHIRE TALE as I was born in York within the sound of the Minster's great St Peter bell which would always be rung at noon and whose boom could be heard for miles around. I was educated at one of Yorkshire's most famous schools and came back from university to work in one of Yorkshire's most famous manufacturing companies, Rowntree and Company Ltd.

This is a multi-faceted tale to reflect a multi-faceted life. I had two quite distinct careers. One as a Marketing Executive at Rowntree where I started in 1955 as a trainee, and left in 1974 as one of the two Marketing Directors for the UK confectionery business on the Divisional Board, to become the Member of Parliament for Pudsey at the General Election in February 1974. I retained that seat through a period of 23$\frac{1}{2}$ years, being returned to Parliament on each of six occasions with an increased majority. My motivation as an MP was rather mixed. I still believed that membership of the House of Commons was a high form of public service and it should not become the fiefdom of so-called 'professional' politicians alone. The Chairman of Rowntree was right when he said that I had got to learn to earn my own living and find out what the world was all about before I could properly represent constituents. I only wished to stand for a Yorkshire seat and it was to some extent because of that it took me so long to find an appropriate seat with the possibility of inheriting a Conservative majority from a well-respected retiring Member. I also believed that the Conservative Party did not have nearly sufficient representatives who were drawn from the ranks of manufacturing industry and management, but the need was certainly pressing with the developing UK role within the European Community. However, as I quickly found, there were other issues which were particularly relevant to Pudsey. This seat was one of the old borough seats of the West Riding of Yorkshire; indeed their Charter was granted by Queen Victoria in 1901, shortly before she died. The creation of this borough provided a major focus for the community in Pudsey who voted for a Council to look after their local affairs. Shortly before I was adopted for Pudsey in December 1972, Mr Heath's Conservative Government had introduced new reforms for local government, including the abolition of the borough seats in places like Leeds and Bradford and the creation of Metropolitan Cities and Metropolitan Counties too. This was apparently based on the belief that the creation of larger local authorities would become attractive for businessmen and others to become councillors in which to manage these very large and somewhat unwieldy businesses. These appeared to be based on the belief that 'Big is Beautiful'. I strongly oppose this and believe, like Dr Schumacher, the German economist, that 'Small is Beautiful' and at 5' 3" I had a right to hold that view. As a result of the revision of local authority boundaries as well as the abolition of the status of boroughs, the local people in the Pudsey community lost a cherished right and a cherished duty to vote in councillors who would take a very local view of what needed to be done. Eventually, after many years, the Metropolitan Cities and the Metropolitan Counties were quietly abolished when it was recognised that the word 'local' had more or less dropped out of local government and the damage to local credibility had still to be corrected.

Now of course a Labour Government has been elected which would appear to be hell bent on devolving powers on to other and larger local administrations like a Parliament in Scotland and an Assembly in Wales. This has been done without a real reference to the consequences on the national Parliament of these geographical changes. I remain sceptical about devolution as a principle and I certainly remain concerned that the Local Government is being undermined as the nation's forum by a government which seeks to make announcements of policy through newspapers or television and has already reduced the Prime Minister's duty to appear before the House of Commons from two sessions a week to one. It is now proposed to change the voting system to a proportional system which is likely to undermine the connection between the single MP and his constituency. There is talk of people being chosen from a list of candidates by Party label which positively introduces a nonentity into the local voting community. I cannot believe that this is a sensible way of proceeding. A Member of Parliament can respond to many needs and establish a working relationship with his constituents which is seldom to be found in any other administration abroad. These are big issues but now that I have retired it must be for others to solve them.

Giles Shaw
Hovingham *January 2000*

'One of the strands of this place is that its Members are all from different backgrounds. We come from different places and we have different attitudes. That fabric makes this place, a place that has survived for hundreds of years. We must be extremely careful that we do not unpick it in a moment of deep penitence or one of deep-seated madness'.

Sir Giles Shaw, Debate on Standards in Public Life. May 1995.

Acknowledgements

I WOULD LIKE TO THANK my former secretary, Diane Craig, who transcribed many hours of tapes with patience and good humour and also made sense of my illegible handwriting. I would also like to thank Ian Baillie and Barbara Twigg, who dispensed wisdom and good critical advice; and my brother Roger, whose childhood memory was much better than mine.

CHAPTER 1

The Toddler's Tale

MY MOTHER AND FATHER, Hugh and Barbara Shaw, both came from Lancashire, from Manchester and Oldham respectively. Her father was a successful solicitor practising in Radcliffe who came to legal fame when he sued the local railway company for denying access to a public right of way, took the case right up to the House of Lords and won. He was a very keen fell walker in the Lake District and he became one of the founder members of the Rucksack Club which was to stimulate climbing mountains in the Lake District whether roped or otherwise and was largely formed by keen walkers from the Manchester area.

Hugh Shaw met Barbara Pickstone at the Brackenrigg Hotel on the shores of Ullswater. The Pickstone family were ensconced on one of their many walking weekends. He tagged along a bit as he had a rather flashy motor car which was much admired by the Pickstone girls. My father was an engineer by training and became a motor engineer when he returned from the First World War and found that the embryonic motor business was starting to take off. He came to York because a friend of his from the War was also a motor engineer and they decided to pool their gratuities from their service in wartime and start a small business. Initially they bought a lorry and started work as hauliers in the York district under the rather grand title of North Riding Haulage Company, soon to be translated into North Riding Motors Limited. He married Barbara in the early 1920s and persuaded her to come to York from the County Palatine. It thus must be said that my parents were immigrants into Yorkshire from the red rose county, not perhaps the best of selection but I had little to do with it.

Settling in York in a house in Stockton Lane, my mother soon found time on her hands. In fact she quickly came to the conclusion that York was a fairly uncultured sort of spot and looked around for further amusement. She became friendly with several members of the York Repertory Company who put on a very good selection of plays to maintain an active theatre for the benefit of the citizens of York. One of the members of this company was a certain Miss Evelyn whose father, Dr Evelyn, and his wife were two of York's most cultivated individuals. Mrs Evelyn was a leading light in the Shakespeare reading club for ladies in York whose members were sufficiently cultivated to pass an interview to establish their credentials. With the support of Mrs Evelyn's daughter, Barbara Shaw joined the Shakespeare reading club and frankly never looked back. When her second son was born Barbara received a small ditty from Miggins Evelyn which ran as follows:

> John Giles Dunkerley Shaw
> Came into this world as his mother soon saw
> He was not what she wanted, she wanted much more
> A Joanne Gillian Dunkerley Shaw.

When in later years I found out about this I was really rather put out. In fact I would say it was a thoroughly undesirable welcome which made me feel positively unwanted. And yet my mother exhibited this little ditty in one of the bedrooms where it remained for many many years. Some six months after my birth she produced a version of *Midsummer Night's Dream* in the local memorial hall at Huntington and Roger, my elder brother by four years, became one of the fairies, being of a suitable age and appearance. I suspect he was Cobweb but he might just have been Mustard Seed.

Whatever his actual role was the fairies were a fairly motley lot drawn from the village children, and one of them gave Roger a present of whooping cough which he brought gallantly back home and gave to his younger brother. This had a profound effect and after a period of being ill, pneumonia was added. I thus spent a long time in bed with frequent visits from a certain Dr Hewitt who for some reason I could never understand was known as Chin Hewitt. Various vapours were smoked in order to allow me to breathe more easily and thus after a long period in bed I was able to recover from this double blow and show sufficient stamina to get up and play a part in an unknown world.

My mother's theatrical ambition moved a stage further when the following year she persuaded the Women's Institutes of Yorkshire to stage another production of *Midsummer Night's Dream* in the City's Museum Garden. It was an open air event of some magnitude and was attended by two of the patrons of the Women's Institute, namely the Princess Royal (Countess of Harewood) and His Grace the Archbishop of York. In addition my mother took the lead part of Puck and rushed about the bushes in the Museum Gardens casting his jocular spells. The only memory that was brought back from this farrago was someone who overheard the Princess Royal leaning over and asking the Archbishop, 'Tell me, Dr Temple, where does Puck go to school?' His Grace's answer was not audible, sad to say. So it could be said that my early life was stricken by outside events and that in the end I became really rather a feeble and undersized youth. This meant that my mother took slightly better care of me and on the whole I got through the early stages of my life as a somewhat shorter and lighter individual than those around of comparable age. However, time moved on and I got better and started running about and looking at the various things that I had missed.

One of the things we observed, my brother and I, was that there were a large number of people living in the village who were soldiers and veterans of the First World War. This was noticeable by the fact that several of them had wooden legs and one or two had metal callipers attached to their legs where they had been wounded. It could be a somewhat frightening sight but on the whole they were very nice people who were affected in this way. Mr Neilson, who ran the little village shop at the corner had clearly suffered in this manner. He used to get on his bicycle with a wonderful squeak which we heard coming and knew, therefore, that his son Jonah might be in charge of the shop and thus more liberal with the spare sweets and peppermints, which were usually scattered around the place.

Huntington, which is a village outside York, was a very pleasant place to grow up. Apart from the sweet shop on the corner it had three other shops, one of which was a bakery and the smell of fresh bread was readily available to those who sneaked around the corner. There were three farms in the village which underline how close it was to the outskirts of York and into the countryside. The most important of these to me was Hall Farm down the little lane by the church, the home of the cows which produced the milk for our house and most other houses. This was the province of Mr Charles Tuthill, the milkman, who regularly gave us lifts down to the farm where we would see the milk being prepared, and the little stamping machine shoving cardboard discs into the top of the bottles, which were then loaded into a lovely horse-drawn trap. The ride back up the village street with dear old Mr Tuthill was a memory which remained with me for a very long time. He was a kindly man and he had a family of several sons, one of whom became the builder's assistant who was employed in later years when alterations took place in the family home at Grey Willows.

Another legacy of the War was that quite a number of people lived in Huntington who had military rank. Next door there was Colonel Cole who was now the chief of the LNER railway police, and as his name was Shenton Cole he was called Shunting Shenton. He had an absolutely gorgeous daughter called Pamela who really was a bit out of our range but we took an intense interest in the beautiful Pamela and she eventually married a chap called Patrick Cave-Brown-Cave. Now how about that for a name? He was, needless to say, a man who worked in the BBC.

Round the corner, beyond A.B. Watson the bakers, was Lieutenant Colonel Henry Wellington Palmer DSO. He was by far the most military gentleman in the village with a nice clipped moustache and a military manner. He organised Armistice Day with commendable efficiency and large quantities of soldiers blowing trumpets duly marched through the village down to the church. He also organised games of croquet in later years, and we all learned to play under his very sharp tutelage until we fell foul of the rules and were occasionally shoved off the lawn. His son, Willie Palmer, despite having a gammy leg from polio, was one of the most important influences on my brother and me because he was always getting up to

Morris car.

pranks and mischief and creating mayhem. But he also had other contacts and one day he suggested we all go down to the knacker's yard where one of the old horses from Palmer's stable, Barney by name, was due to be shot. He thought it rather an exciting operation; I frankly was sick and ran away from it.

Down Church Lane, at West Huntington Hall was Major Raymond Quirke. He had an ancient Morris car with a great big dicky seat, and nothing was more exciting than the arrival of Major Quirke early in the morning to take me down to the kindergarten school in the next village. The car had a wonderful horn which was attached at the side with a nice balloon in rubber to squeeze and grip to our hearts' content. His son, Desmond Quirke became a very valuable chum. He was always getting into hot water of one kind or another. He was the one who always left his sandwiches behind on expeditions and who was bullied unmercifully by Willie Palmer who used to do things like throw his sandwiches into the pond and called him 'Ripen' when he blushed. It was believed that the sandwiches were made of bloater paste which was a fairly indifferent commodity. His mother Dorothy had extremely short sight and was once spotted by Willie Palmer in Woolworth's with her nose covered in flour. She had got a bit too close to the counters.

I suppose I should also mention that my father was 'through the War' as they say. He was a motor engineer by trade and a very keen motorcyclist before the War, including time spent on rallies in various parts of the Lake District. It was not surprising, therefore, that he was drafted into the unit known as the 57th Divisional Signal Company of the Royal Engineers which included dispatch riding as one of its main activities. He very rarely spoke about his exploits and was extremely embarrassed by the fact that he had a large number of campaign medals on a long pin which were designed to be worn on military occasions. He dismissed this as stuff that came up with the rations and frankly I never saw him wear them at Remembrance Day, but he did have a memento which he kept rather secretively in one of his drawers. This took the form of a piece of brass taken from a shell case which had been hammered into the shape of a cigarette case and was clearly made in the trenches. It contained inside all the signatures of the men in the dispatch riders' troop, including himself. On the front it had one name only which was ARRAS, commemorating one of the battlefields on which he served.

North Riding Motors was his business and it offered for sale a wonderful range of some of the great cars of the day. The Morgan plus 4, the Armstrong Siddeley, the Rover and the Jowett were names across the front of the building. In those days it was the engineering of the motor cars which provided the competition and the interest in buying. They were all different, they were all specially hand built and they were all fairly expensive except for the Jowett from Bradford. But to my father they represented the best engineering that the British motor industry could provide. The business was started in the early 1920s and went right through the Second World War until the late 1950s. Many of the cars of course had fallen by the wayside by then and the business very nearly went under when the great Jowett Javelin, introduced in the 1950s, folded up because the Ford Motor Company bought the body supplier of the Javelin. However Volkswagen were on the lookout for a dealer and my brother who had joined the firm and who spoke perfect German found himself going to Wolfsburg and other places in pursuit of the ideal salesmanship for the famous 'Beetle'.

CHAPTER 2

The Family's Tale

MIDWAY DURING THE 1930s, in 1935 to be precise, two major events occurred. First the monarch, King George V and his good Queen Mary celebrated their Silver Jubilee. This event was marked by a distribution of memorial mugs to children of reasonable age at the Hall in Huntington. I am not certain but I think I managed to get one although I don't think it lasted the course. The second was that my parents decided to go on a holiday by car to Europe, in particular to southern Germany. I should perhaps mention that my mother had been educated in Germany, living with a German family in Berlin (after the First World War was over) and also with a family in Switzerland in order to improve her French. But on this occasion it was entirely holiday and I think the team included my mother, my father, my mother's younger sister Sheila and an old travelling companion of the Shaw family, Mr Dennis Lawton. You will note there was no reference to my brother or me and I had to check up with my brother as to who on earth was looking after us during this long period of absence. I think the answer was our maternal grandmother. It was possibly because of this trip that when my mother came back after an idyllic time, and despite the sight of lorryloads of Nazi soldiers, she persuaded my father to agree to a major decision in her life.

She resolved to take part in local government and to offer herself for election to the Flaxton Rural District Council. Although it was rural by name, it was so called because it was not part of an urban community. It was nevertheless one of the larger district councils of its kind and its authority ran in a semi-circle around York itself, taking in a great number of the rural villages including Huntington, New Earswick and Haxby. This meant that at the elections in 1936 she became a candidate and the Armstrong Siddeley tourer was covered with large posters saying 'Vote for Shaw'. I have to confess a modest tingling sensation about this election. It did seem rather exciting from a very lowly position in the back of the car and when it grew to a climax at election day things called rosettes were widely worn. No doubt, because of the elegant language in which my mother addressed her potential constituents, she was handsomely elected. I should make it clear in passing that she did not stand on any occasion under a party label. If she had a political taste it was for the Liberal Party which was the traditional party of Methodists and which her mother, our grandmother, very strongly espoused.

Be that as it may, the consequence of the Flaxton Rural District Council was not lost on the children. Meetings were held in York at odd times of the day, important people came to visit like Mr Leslie Parker, the sanitary inspector, and on one extra-special occasion my mother was host at the opening ceremony for the new Haxby Sewage Works which I think the great Mr Walter Elliot, Minister for Health had come to open, possibly to fill or possibly to empty. There was much toing and froing and much chat about the actions of the Council and above all of the people who were the Councillors. It seemed that in those days the power of local government was quite considerable and the relationship between local government and local people was much greater than it is today. It is probably too great a coincidence to say that it was this sort of experience that encouraged me towards a political career. More likely it was this experience which indicated to me that local politics was now a fact of family life and that it appeared to have a degree of importance.

Meanwhile, my father was busy with other matters, including, of course, the fairly extensive development of the North Riding Motor Company in the sale and maintenance of cars. He was not without some skill in architecture and he helped to design a house which he was able to build on the shores of Ullswater Lake in the Lake District. This was a major undertaking, at some distance, but he longed to have a rural retreat and no doubt the advent of local politics had something to do with the distance that he chose. By 1937 the family Lakeland holiday home had been completed and we visited with some frequency. My brother certainly got much benefit from

The author's mother, Councillor Irene Barbara Shaw, 1934.

The author's father with brother Roger, after a successful day, 1937.

The author showing an interest in drains, age 5 years.

this, but I rather less because the excitement of fell walking and hill climbing was more in his domain than mine. Meanwhile, I plodded on at Kate Wood's Kindergarten and steadily the time grew closer for major decisions on the next phase of education. My brother had already gone to a school in Cheshire which had been attended by at least two members of my mother's family, the Pickstones, whose home was in Manchester.

As the possibility of war arose preparations were also made at Grey Willows itself. The garden yielded a large hole which became an air-raid shelter built by Reg Todd and his happy team who sang 'Little Sir Echo' with prodigious repetition. It was then decided that part of the stable block should be converted to the village ARP Headquarters. My father immediately became the Chief Air-Raid Warden and my mother, with a suitable white tin hat, deigned to become his deputy. It meant more activity, more excitement and more distraction from Kate Wood's Kindergarten. It seemed natural that I should join my brother at his prep school in Cheshire and at least my father argued that it was not a bad idea to attend a school far away from bombing, unlike York which was fairly close to the city of Hull. I think this view was strengthened by the fact that boys from Hull, particularly the bombed quarters of the city, were being evacuated to York and other places and evacuees carrying their gas masks in the appropriate manner became a feature of local villages.

We took two of these into the back premises at Grey Willows which was hastily formed into a bedsitter. Their names were Frank and Dennis and I think they stayed for a short time, although I don't think their company was an asset to our activities.

Mostyn House School in Cheshire was a real eye-opener. It was equipped with everything that a boy would like to have – a room full of trains, a billiard room, a huge gym, an indoor playground and plenty of outdoors for organised games of all kinds. As was typical for prep schools of that time, and all other schools for that matter, it was essential to bring teachers out of retirement to take the place of those who had joined up and gone to the War. In this particular regard Mostyn House was very fortunate, in that there were three of outstanding quality. First, Mr Low, a big heavily built man whose experience in the First World War resulted in him picking shrapnel out of his hands which were clasped behind his back during active dissertation on Latin matters. It was a keen competition to be able to have a look at the shrapnel before it was dropped into the litter bin which after lessons was thoroughly searched for wicked fragments.

The second was Mr H.B.F. Kenny who came to teach history; he had lost his leg in the First World War and a replacement was affixed to him. I remember his vivid use of a large map cast in plaster form which set out the whole of mainland Europe. On this he could deploy with some accuracy the lines of Russian advances or German retreats in Russia and lessons always included an update of the doings of Marshal Rokossovsky or Marshal Koniev. The battle of Stalingrad was vividly depicted in this way. But the master who had most influence on me in this phase was Mr J.L.P. Cort whose subjects included botany, biology and the wild outdoors, and any other aspects of natural history.

Visit to Dr Cohen.

The school was well equipped with the complete collection of birds' eggs bequeathed by Sir Wilfred Grenfell, the Labrador explorer and these were housed in a small room in the school grounds which became the focus of environmental activity as we would call it today. But J.L.P. Cort was more than that. He took out expeditions and walks and nearly every day we found some new aspect of botany or entomology; caterpillars were caught and bred in jars, ants were encased in a glass wall case. I remember a wormery showing them tunnelling merrily, flat against the glass, and many ponds were scoured for newts, frogs and toads etc. He was enthusiastic beyond measure and could be heard shouting to the crocodile of small boys that followed, 'Look, here is *bombus terrestris*, the common humble bee.' 'This is the common frog *rana temporaria*; never confuse it with the edible frog which is *rana esculenta*.' I found all this excitement and exploration to be very appealing and I became thoroughly immersed in wild life and particularly birds, aided and abetted by the arrival of Romany books which were first published in 1940. My grandmother presented me with one each year as they were published. They were a very favourite and influential guide to natural history. The school also provided very good services in looking after small boys in this formative phase. However, my father one day received a letter from the Headmaster which said in as many words, 'We rather think that Giles is not growing sufficiently and may be in need of clinical examination. I recommend that we go to a learned Professor in Birkenhead named Cohen who I think should examine him.' The first thing I knew was that I was summoned to the Headmaster with the information that we were going to Birkenhead to see a doctor. In due course we were ushered in to the consulting room of this eminent man and I was introduced to Dr Cohen. He then stripped me off to my bare essentials which under the Headmaster's gaze was not the happiest of conditions and promptly produced a glass vessel, gave it to me and said, 'Empty your bladder.' Frankly I had never heard of a bladder whether full or empty. I knew not, so I spat in the vessel and handed it back. This caused the Headmaster to explode and he roughly took me behind a crude screen, shoved my genitals into the vessel and said 'Pee in it, you fool.' My excitement was intense of course and I damned nearly overflowed the vessel which was rapidly passed back to Professor Cohen with beaded bubbles winking at the brim, full of the true, the blushful Hippocrene as Keats so aptly put it. The result of this amazing experience was a whole lot of powders which I had to take in the morning and in the evening under the supervision of matron. I am not certain that anything helpful in terms of growth came out of this episode but I was pleased to note that Professor Cohen ultimately became Lord Cohen of Birkenhead and a leader in his profession.

Plays were produced at the school and I remember my brother who maintained the lead over me of four sublime years taking a part in *Bardell v Pickwick* and also as Toad in *Toad of Toad Hall.* I suspect I might have been the baby in *Bardell v Pickwick.*

As war became closer the school made preparations for a very large underground shelter to be built so that most of the school could be accommodated overnight on racks of bunks. This brought an entirely new excitement into school life and a competition to see who had got the most striking siren suit and other exotic gear. Nevertheless, the proximity of Liverpool and Birkenhead did mean that many nights were spent in the air-raid shelter and it was a colossal boon to the school's attraction for parents. In 1942 my brother and I were back at Grey Willows when the one great air attack on York took place. My mother and father, whom you will recall were warden and deputy warden of the Huntington ARP post, forgot all about the air-raid shelter and enjoyed watching the bombs drop on York station and some of the streets – only when the raid was over did they remember us and rushed up to our bedroom to see if we were all right. This total failure of parental duty did not pass unrecorded for future use!

CHAPTER 3

The Schoolboy's Tale

THERE WERE TWO MORE ISSUES in Mostyn House School which are worth reporting on. First the Headmaster's decision to broaden the range of school honours that could be awarded. He was, I think, mindful of the fact that a lot of people in civilian occupations were being awarded honours and he felt it only reasonable that those who were not playing cricket or rugby or football might, if they achieved greatness, be included in the honours list. It thus fell to my lot as a keen gardener to be awarded my first XI colours for a particularly pleasant display of good vegetables, many of which were subsequently consumed in the school dining room. I have to say in all modesty that this was not the prize I would have looked for but it was in fact the only prize that I was probably capable of winning. However, I very nearly won the writing prize, not for a volume of prose or any other work of art but for the passage of poetry which was set that year to be written out in the school's strict script. No letters were to be joined together, no letters were to be transcribed in cursive, and all letters were to be displayed in their full intact size and shape in meticulous fashion. This style of writing was particularly useful in assisting spelling and the like but it was a damned nuisance if you had to take notes in lessons subsequently. Needless to say you were not allowed to take notes in Mostyn House classes unless they were in the school script. However, I failed to win this prize although my effort was considered very worthy indeed and I came second to the Headmaster's daughter – I wonder if that was a coincidence?

The other issue which the Headmaster engaged in was an attempt to prevent my father sending me on to Sedbergh where my brother Roger was already established. He made the case on two grounds: i) I clearly was not of a size suitable for the main games of Sedbergh School such as rugby and he doubted very much if they would have me; ii) if I was considered suitable he felt I would be mercilessly bullied and my life would be a perfect misery. Once more, therefore, the size issue came to the fore and despite the efforts of the newly ennobled Lord Cohen of Birkenhead my future was to be hazarded virtually on this account alone. My father took me over to be interviewed by the Headmaster at Sedbergh so that I could satisfy myself that it wasn't the den of bullying that my prep school had believed. The Headmaster was a twinkling-eyed chap but a fairly taciturn Scot. His wife, however, was much more influential. She was a keen bird watcher and immediately took me on a tour of the garden to observe where a host of birds could nest and described to me also the access to the fells around Sedbergh which was already famous for its range of raptors and other birds. As access to the fells was not barred but encouraged it seemed to me a considerable gain. Finally, when my father asked if due to my small size I would be at risk on the rugby field the wise old Headmaster replied, 'It should be up to his Housemaster to determine. Knowing his Housemaster as I do he has the interest of all boys in his house at heart and he would allow no such thing.' In actual fact he was as good as his word and I did not play rugby for the first term. I suspect the Headmaster at Mostyn House ultimately ate humble pie when he heard that I had won the 10-mile fell race at Sedbergh in 1949, known as the Long Run.

The end of my final term at Mostyn House coincided with the first day of results coming in from the General Election of 1945. My father drove over in one of his splendid Rover saloons and as a little extra excitement he brought my grandmother with him, picked up in Manchester for the return journey to York. Joy wasn't entirely overflowing at her presence, not just because she had an ancient fur coat which was slightly *de trop* on a September day but largely because as a long-term Liberal she began to weep profusely as the results came in and more and more Liberals lost their seats. Finally she was in a flood of tears at the disappearance at the hustings of Mr Clement Davies, the leader of the Liberal Party and as good a Methodist as she was. It was gloom throughout the family and throughout the day, a pretty poor homecoming I would say. There was, however, a major compensation – the wartime restrictions on petrol had really prevented my father from enjoying the amenity of Glencoyne, his house at Ullswater, and he was sadly unable to get there very much. This involved the house being tenanted and as the War proceeded the tenant got more and more anxious, being a London resident, to have an extended tenancy and virtually wanted to live up there. Eventually my parents decided that it might be a sensible idea to sell the house to her provided we had included in the contract the right of the first refusal if she was proposing to sell at any time. After the disposal of the house at Ullswater, my father was on the lookout for something else and in 1942 found a property between Broughton-in-Furness and Coniston. This was a very different dwelling set in a very pleasant valley but of course no access to a lake other than the 8 miles to Coniston. However it did provide a fabulous garden and a lot of excellent countryside which was full of birds ranging from buzzards to bullfinches. This was ideal territory for me and with the arrival of one of my school friends as support during the summer holidays we set about trying to discover nature's bounty around the house which was known as Hawthwaite How.

As it was now late September the birds had long since given up raising young and building nests etc. but the garden was particularly full of birds' nests from the previous spring. My chum and I decided on the possibility of making a collection of birds' nests which could not only provide evidence of the range of breeding birds in the place but might be of value in itself in so far as we had never known of a collection of birds' nests being made available for viewing. We quickly found nests of long-tailed tits, flycatchers, bullfinches, willow and garden warblers, ring ousels from up the fell, jays, tree creepers and many others. With deft fingers and not a little trouble we actually extracted them from crevices, trees and holes in the bark in which they were located and transferred them gently to a very large black oak chest which was at one end of the drawing room in the house. In fact we very soon more than half covered the floor of this particular chest and we had to lay cardboard to provide a structure for a second layer. In this we laid nests of rather different quality like housemartins and swallows and one or two larger items like half a magpie's nest – it was too large a structure to go into the chest – and a black-backed gull's nest which was rather a large contrivance but could be handled with a fair amount of roughness as it was far from delicate.

This took us quite a bit of time and we greatly enjoyed the search and retrieval and the development of the collection. As Sandy Campbell, my friend, was only available for a short period of time, when he departed a lot of the fun departed with him and as we had nicely filled the chest I soon got weary of doing this thing on my own and I left it at that.

I have to say that it was some years later that the chest was opened and my mother had a fit when she saw the massive cobwebs and other signs of insectoral activity spread across the chest and a whole lot of rotting vegetation and various other detritus festooning the bottom of the chest. It was in retrospect rather a ham-fisted exercise, but I was saddened that so much time had been spent on retrieving so many excellent specimens only to have them destroyed by the internal activity of bugs within the chest. A lesson learned, a bonfire made and I resolved to study birds in their wild environment at every opportunity. The first opportunity that beckoned was Sedbergh School.

I joined Lupton House at Sedbergh as one of seven new boys in September 1945. Amazingly I knew one of them, Bill Byrd, whose father was the doctor at Glen Ridding where my father's house Glencoyne had been built. He had the right name and he was a keen birdman himself. Archie Turnbull from Alnwick was a keen photographer and came along willingly on expeditions looking for birds around Sedbergh. In fact, the seven of us banded together quite quickly and as new boys are wont to do found much solace in our own company, dealing with the issues that new boys face at the start of a new period at a major boarding school. This developed over time and we recorded our activities both in the classroom and in the countryside; when we reached our 50th anniversary we agreed to leave our Annals, as they were called, to the School Archivist for safekeeping. I suspect they may still be viewed, for those who want to know how seven fairly different young boys turned over time into seven fairly accomplished young men.

The 'Big 7', Sedbergh School, 1945-50. Standing: Byrd, Turnbull;
Sitting: Dodds, Shaw, Spinney; Front: MacInnes, Gardner.

The first thing I found having been excused rugby for the term was that the emphasis moved away from the rugby field to the roads and lanes around Sedbergh. On wet days running was the order of the day and on some occasions house runs, when all the boys in the house would be formed into packs and run through fixed distances. This was the only form of exercise available when the rugby fields were sodden with water. Water and Sedbergh go together very easily. Sedbergh town is located at the confluence of the River Dee, the River Rawthey and the River Clough, or as the school song puts it 'where Clough and Dee and Rawthey come singing from the hills'. The climate was distinctly wet and rainfall was well above average, I would guess.

Running around the hills or along the lanes was a fairly well-practised exercise which was by no means discouraged. I am convinced that this ultimately led to my interest in running in the 10-mile race when I was old enough to do so. Running over the fells to look for buzzards' nests or peregrine falcons' eyries, following the call of the raven or looking with care for that very elusive bird the merlin, all this made running worthwhile even if one was bored with the distances involved.

Sedbergh was indeed a birdwatcher's paradise as was proved by the Reverend Ingram Cleasby's book which has chronicled many decades of Sedbergh boys and Sedbergh birds and was published in 1999. In addition to running round the fells looking out for birds Sedbergh had much more activity to offer the seven new boys at Lupton House in 1945. We took to fives and some of us took to squash. We favoured fives because it could provide a foursome game and I, in particular, being so small was able to duck and avoid the ball more often than others. We were taught by the Reverend Austin Boggis and on some occasions the Housemaster himself, I. Christopherson, who was the Captain of Boats at Worcester College, Oxford, before being appointed to Sedbergh to run the cricket. We always wondered why he came, but he was a very good teacher of most things including English and Latin.

In 1947 there came the great freeze which resulted in the house, and indeed the school, running out of fuel and the government more or less running out of fuel for the nation. Rapid plans were laid to cancel lessons in the school buildings and have them in the houses so that coal and coke could be conserved and the heating of the vast spaces of Victorian classrooms avoided. Lupton House had fairly primitive ablutions and the main toilet block was outside in the yard. It caused some amusement when the urinals gradually froze up and there were large and long yellow icebergs adorning parts of the building but at least we made our contribution to saving fuel.

Then there was music and concerts. My father believed that the school offered a first term free tuition for musical instruments and I was, therefore, asked what I would like to learn. I opted for the flute believing it to be pretty similar to the penny whistle and, therefore, easy to play. I was appointed to a teacher called Mrs Whiteside, known throughout the school as Madame Côte Blanche and after a fortnight of trying to say 'twice two' into a small orifice at the end of a horizontal ebony pipe I was found completely wanting. My father received a report which said: 'I regret to say that Giles's mouth is the wrong shape for the flute.' He also got a bill for 5 guineas which he felt rather aggrieved about but he was reminded by a letter from the Headmaster that the musical instruments to be offered free were stringed instruments, so music was off.

Then came acting. Each year houses produced a play for the benefit of the audience in the school and sometimes there were school productions of Gilbert and Sullivan works. Having been proved a non-musician my chances of taking part in operatic works were slim, but the producer of *HMS Pinafore* felt that to be able to hit the right note I could be taught to count and most of the songs allocated to Sir Joseph Porter were pretty ordinary compositions. I was, therefore, selected for the part and spent most of my time rehearsing patter songs. In the end I was able to count quickly enough and to come in frequently enough to be able to master this form of musicianship. I was intrigued to know that the part of Sir Joseph Porter was based upon the actual career of one W.H. Smith who from running the family business as a national bookseller was quickly translated into high office as First Lord of the Admiralty. The production of this opera gave me a very good opportunity to take an interest in the stage and a number of productions followed. We also combined and produced sketches for the house concert party which occurred at the end of the summer or winter terms and was designed to point fun at the school's institutions and its characters. I was a very cheeky writer of verse and doggerel and we got away with a lot of punchy lines which were well recognised amongst the audience. The Lupton House concert was regularly attended by a wide selection of people from other houses to find out how we could get away with it all without causing a fuss. Making fun in a concert party was less important in one's school career than actually getting the work done. School reports were not very encouraging on this matter and my mother got a bit touchy that I was wasting too much of my time on non-essentials. One of my big problems turned out to be illegible writing. Bearing in mind I was taught at Mostyn House to write in legible and well-spelled script and that joined up lettering was anathema, I was at a great disadvantage. However, I made an effort and in particular I noted that my problem was the speed at which I wrote rather than its legibility. Happily I got it right just in time for the School Certificate Exam and the problem was significantly reduced by the time I had reached Higher Certificate.

My first entry into the 10-mile fell race was in 1949. This was keenly contested amongst about seventy boys and there were points awarded for places gained which contributed to the inter-house sports cup competition. There was a medical examination to ensure that nobody was going to die en route, and there was quite a lot or organised training to ensure that the teams from houses were well enough prepared.

It appeared from some of the timings during the trials that I was performing fairly well, but the problems of the course were threefold. One, there was quite a lot of straight fell running up and down the ghylls as they appeared; then there was quite a lot of crossing the moor with thick heather and other obstacles which made for heavy going; finally, there was some 3 miles of hard plodding along the road to arrive at the finishing line which was just round the library corner after quite a considerable pull up Punches Hill. It was very important, therefore, to time the various stages at a sensible level so that cumulatively you had enough stamina left for the long road patch and could determine whether you should be faster there or should put your main effort into the fell. I was extremely lucky to be a very slight boy, with low weight but reasonable stamina and as the day dawned it was clearly going to be bright and dry with a reasonably hot sun. The ideal Sedberghians were tall and hefty lads used to the first XV rugby and somewhat unused to running a race of this scale in what turned out to be summer heat. In consequence, many of them dropped out or slowed up during the course of the race but I found myself bouncing along merrily amongst the leaders during the first stage. It is traditional to view the race from various vantage points some distance away from it because the hills and fells easily hide the runners. Because I was so small I was not spotted amongst the leaders for quite some time and this all added to the excitement when I suddenly appeared in second place at Danny Bridge, ready to face the 3 miles on the road back to Sedbergh. I remember one of the local bystanders when he observed me coming up the hill from the bridge shouting out 'God bless his little legs' from which I assumed he had a wager on at the Black Bull which might benefit from my arriving first. I did arrive first in the pretty slow time of 1 hour and 19 minutes. The record for the race I hasten to say was about 1 hour 12 minutes at that time. However, winning the 10-mile is considered to be one of the foremost prizes available in the school and although one is not presented with a piece of silver or its equivalent I was awarded my House and School colours by the end of the day.

It was not long before the dreadful thought dawned on me that I would be eligible to run in the race in 1950 and no doubt the market place would feel that I was eligible to win it again. It is a most uncomfortable position to be in and happily all my chums gathered round and decided that the right thing to do was to go off and do something quite different, to spend the summer term photographing birds or something and go for a holiday abroad and not consider running round the fells until January 1950, some two months before the race. Certainly Bill Byrd and I had fun photographing lapwings on Frost Row during the summer term and made some progress. My parents were considering taking the car abroad to France and Switzerland and this proved to be a great excitement. The car was the redoubtable Jowett Javelin, a relatively new car outside Britain and a somewhat ticklish one to drive over long distances unless you were prepared to do running repairs. Sadly, the problem turned out to be rather worse than that in that the Jowett Javelin was a fairly delicate instrument when it came to petrol and carburettors. The Continent was full of fairly dodgy petrol, post-war utilities making their mark. When approaching the Alps we started to have trouble with the carburettor and the garagiste where we stopped and looked at the Jowett Javelin with a somewhat wild eye when he found the engine mounted in front of the front axle and designed as a flat four with the cylinders horizontally opposed. 'Démontez la pompe' was the cry and H.D. Shaw looked on aghast. However, we did get to Switzerland and we stayed with a family which my mother had stayed with after the First World War. With a chalet by Lake Neuchatel we quickly forgot about the Jowett engine. Nevertheless, it was obvious that my father was concerned all the way back until we reached the safety of the United Kingdom.

The summer term also brought other matters of great importance to the fore – the question of the Higher School Certificate Exams and university entry, and the beginnings of an interest in the school cadet force, bearing in mind that we were all due for two years' National Service in September 1950. It was extremely good that the majority of those in our band of 1945 who wanted to go to university chose Cambridge. In fact, three of us chose St John's College – Neville Spinney, Rodney Dodds and myself – and one of us, David MacInnes chose Jesus College. In those days certain university colleges offered special arrangements with leading public schools such as closed exhibitions, which tended to be awarded on merit and the recommendation of the Headmaster, aided and abetted by the Entrance Examination to the University. The system had all the features of the Judge's appointment in *Trial by Jury*, namely it was managed by a job, and a good job too! However, that modest ordeal was a little way off.

The year 1950 was the final one for all of us and we set out to make the best of it. I think on the whole we did. We had some excellent expeditions to the fells, birding was good and a curlew was photographed in the nest, and we all gained our Higher Certificates and the appropriate entry to the relevant universities and colleges. I was awarded an exhibition to St John's under the splendid title of the 'Lupton and Hebblethwaite Exhibition'. It was worth all of £52.00 per year much to my father's chagrin. David MacInnes was head of Lupton House and head of the school. I trained reasonably hard for the 10-mile race and was rewarded by the race being held once again in high summer temperatures. I duly huffed and puffed my way around and found, once again, that it was easier for a slender lightweight to complete the course than for those of larger and heavier frame. And so we gathered for the concert in the evening which concluded with all the entrants for the race coming up in order of arrival at the finishing point and I suppose for the winner this was the most moving part of the entire day. I moved up to the stage through a standing, cheering ovation and stood alone for a short time before the others gradually came up to fill the stage, bearing in mind that something like seventy or eighty people took part. We then all sang the school song 'The Long Run' and tears were quietly shed, although Sedberghians are not meant to blub in public. The summertime brought *HMS Pinafore* and Sir Joseph Porter duly strutted his stuff. I must confess I enjoyed this hugely – whether it was the public acclaim, or whether it was the sheer joy of participating in one of Gilbert's most charming operettas, I don't know. At the same time as rehearsing all this we had to come to terms with the requirements of National Service.

CHAPTER 4

The Trooper's Tale

I NEVER ENJOYED THE DISCIPLINES of the gymnasium very much
and for a long time our RQMS Ernest Stoker had recognised that
I was a fairly weak offering. In fact I remember him shouting whilst I
was trying to get my 'insteps to the bar': 'Shaw, Shaw you are so weak
I think you should go to a rehabitulation centre.' He probably meant
a rehabilitation centre, but the effect on me was just the same.
Certainly marching in full pack, plus all the drilling that is required
in a cadet force was somewhat alien to my way of life. However, I
obtained the great Certificate Part II and thus took my first hesitant
step towards the War Office Selection Board for officers and
gentlemen. September 1950 saw me making entry to Catterick Camp
in Yorkshire where I was due to set out for basic training with the
17th/21st Lancers. How well I remember those first few days in this
entirely alien environment. We all queued up for 'jabs' on Day One.
We were all stripped to the waist and slowly went forward until we
reached the screen where the inoculation team was waiting with
injection needles at the ready – sabres drawn. One great big chap
came out from behind the curtain and a voice from the back of the
queue said, 'What's it like, Lofty?' He replied, 'There's fook-all to it'
and collapsed in a heap. That ensured there was panic in the ranks.

The discipline of the barrack room with 'parade's at eight o'clock,
but thems as is keen gets fell in previous', and inspections by
sergeants: 'What's this under your bed Shaw?' 'Dust,' I said. 'If the
medical officer were here and he stood where I'm standing he would
say that was a festering heap which could well presage an outbreak of
cholera with hundreds dead by the morning. Get it shifted!'
22405273 Trooper Shaw J.G.D. duly got it shifted in quick time.

Those first few weeks of military life were eye-opening for all of us
from whatever stable we had come. Shooting on the ranges, route

marches around the countryside or spending Saturday morning trying to find a silver hip flask which one of the senior officers of the 17th/21st Lancers had accidentally lost whilst shooting in the woods. There was training in the use of firearms and Bren guns, and training in the driving and maintenance of Bedford trucks, which were three-tonners or 15 cwt light vehicles. We learned how to drive them on the roads around Catterick, we learned how to maintain them to a modest degree, and we learned how to repair the various Bren guns and other weapons which the Army provided. We then went off to take the WOSB exam which I found particularly difficult. I got into a real muddle with my team, failed to effect a river-crossing in the due time and practically collapsed from exhaustion. However, they must have been short of officer material that year or perhaps particularly short of short officers.

The consequence of that was that in due time I was posted to the Officer Cadet Training School at Mons Barracks, Aldershot, the venue for all cadets in the Royal Armoured Corps. It is one thing to pass the War Office Selection Board looking for likely officer material, but it is quite another to pass the Officer Cadet Training School which effectively commissions you as an officer. This requires much more soldiering including the classic regime of barrack square bashing and some important exams followed by a major test as an officer in command, which was known in the Armoured Corps as the Trek. All in all I was not exactly elated with the prospect of having to compete in this rather specialist academy! Nor was Aldershot or indeed Hampshire an area of the country with which I had any familiarity whatever.

The simple uniform of the Officer Cadet was in fact the blouse and trousers of the battledress fastened together by a belt which was made of stronger fabric, which was blancoed and brassoed and tightly fastened around the waist. When we moved from Catterick to Aldershot we were required to have new uniforms more befitting in style to an Officer Cadet – a white plastic circle was fitted behind the cap badge for example. There were white tabs on the shoulder straps and I believe a little bit of white on the lapels of those who showed great promise. So we were asked to assemble and RSM Brittain was proposing to inspect every man to see if he was up to the standard of presentation required. He lumbered slowly down the lines with CSM Smythe close behind issuing instructions as to alterations or changes in the way in which the uniform was either made or the way in which the cadet was actually wearing it. As the tallest was on the left and the shortest was on the right it was some time before he approached me but I somehow sensed a total eclipse of the sun as this immense frame lowered over me. He then got out his pace stick, which he normally kept tightly gripped under his arm, and opened it to the width of 3 feet, which was the way of measuring the length of the march pace, prodded it into my thigh and said to CSM Smythe, 'This wants taking in round the fly.' Quite frankly that was an absurdity. The whole uniform needed to be changed, the trousers should be shortened and the blouse should be of a correct size. Eventually all this was done and I got something approaching a new uniform.

My contact with CSM Smythe (of the Irish Guards) was of the more orthodox kind. Drilling on the barrack square was part of the way of maintaining control of the cadets. There could be short drills, long drills, vigorous drills or fairly sedate drills. This seemed to be very much at the whim of the Sergeant Major who was conducting it. Usually we marched with rifles at the shoulder or rifles at the high port or something or other, but rarely were we asked to parade in full kit or FSMO as it was known (field service marching order) which included tin hats, knapsacks, water bottles etc., as if we were on our way to war. It was one of these FSMO drills that brought my undoing with CSM Smythe (of the Irish Guards). He had us all double marking time with FSMO on our backs, sides and fronts and that entailed one literally not moving backwards or forwards but exercising the legs at a frantic speed in order to demonstrate fitness on parade. Frankly I found the weight of all this kit, particularly of the rifle, was beginning to sink me a little, at which point I heard the falsetto tones of CSM Smythe (of the Irish Guards), 'Shaw, Shaw,' he shouted, 'if you bend your knees any more we'll lose you.' This brought a roar of laughter from my colleagues and we virtually stumbled to a halt and finished double marking time. It was a wonderful example of how sergeant majors operate, not only to control the individuals but also to establish a relationship which was not just one of terror but of terror mixed with wicked satire.

The Officer Cadet also had to take lessons about military tactics. He had to have knowledge too of the Army's equipment for fighting purposes and a history lesson on some of the battles fought in the recent war, in order to become familiar with the role of the Infantry in war, together with the role of the Armoured Corps and supporting units like the RASC, the Royal Ordnance Corps and the Royal Signals. In my particular case I was destined to join the 16th/5th Lancers which was a reconnaissance regiment equipped with Daimler armoured cars. The reconnaissance role had long been an historic role of cavalry units so it was not surprising that although cavalry units had long ago abandoned horses as a major arm of fighting, the need for reconnaissance, particularly in areas like the desert was extremely great. The Daimler cars were relatively light in weight, being 7 tonnes, and had an engine which was situated at the back of the vehicle and four-wheel-drive propulsion which allowed it to go as fast forward as it could go backwards (or vice versa). This was done to provide it with not only great mobility but great manoeuvrability so that it could get out of difficult situations if necessary.

CHAPTER 5

The Lancer's Tale

As LUCK WOULD HAVE IT and thanks to the angels of good fortune, I scraped through, not obviously on the results of the Trek but on the cumulative effect of other aspects of the examining process, including the little speech that I had to give to the examining officers on Britain's role in the world today. I suspect I also got some marks from the little ditty I recounted at the Sergeants' Mess party one night. I, therefore, was present for the passing out parade and I was sent down to the headquarters of the Royal Armoured Corps at their barracks in Dorset where I was duly enlisted into the 16th/5th Lancers. At this point, my father, who always had an eye for proper practice, sent me an Orlik pipe and a 2-oz tin of Three Nuns tobacco which he claimed I should rightly enjoy now that I was an officer and I must behave like a gentleman. I remember I started the first puff on the top deck of the bus going to Wareham, not far away from the camp where it ignited and I was very nearly ill inhaling the surrounding smoke. Then followed some blessed leave at home before I was summoned to join the troopship *Devonshire* at Liverpool where I met some good chums who were also going out to join the 16th/5th Lancers. They were Christopher Robinson, Charlie Vincent, John Burton and Nick Barber. The five of us were a bit like the seven who joined Lupton House in 1945. We determined to make our mark and we greatly enjoyed our mutual friendship. Many extremely hilarious incidents took place with one or the other of us during our early military days.

The *Devonshire* was a lumbering vessel which took a considerable time to navigate itself down into the Mediterranean. It called briefly at Cyprus and then went across the water to Port Said. Then it went up the North African coast to the Cyrenaican port of Benghazi. Kitbags and suitcases were disembarked and we were collected by a

3-ton truck for the journey to Barce camp where the 16th/5th Lancers had its headquarters. On arrival we met the Adjutant and others who were going to be concerned with our welfare but we were shocked to discover that we were not all being located in the same place. Nick Barber and Charlie Vincent were allocated to C Squadron which was already on deployment in the Canal Zone, while John Burton and I were allocated to B Squadron which was on detachment in Derna a few hundred miles up the coast. Our happy band of warriors was sharply dispersed and frankly we didn't meet again for a considerable period of time. On balance, John and I thought we had the best deal. Derna was not so far away as to be impossible to connect up with the rest of the Regiment at Barce quite often, in what was known as countryside, whereas the Canal Zone was hardly a pretty place to be, even though there was a high element of expectation and excitement.

Before we moved off, however, we stayed a few days to meet most of the officers, in particular the Colonel, and to be measured up for tropical kit and generally be made welcome amongst the Mess and to learn a bit about what the Regiment's role was and why it had been split up in this way. The Colonel was a charming man, coming towards the end of his time. He had a big, rotund, friendly face with a russet colour which had quite an affinity with Glen Morangie. Our role in Cyrenaica was to try and maintain peace in the country, because the Senussi which formed the largest tribe had frequently caused outbreaks of violence in their search for better lands for grazing. At this point in time oil had not been discovered and therefore we were dealing with a desert kingdom which had few natural resources except agriculture, and had been widely developed by the Italians under Mussolini's regime when they had occupied Libya before the War. The detachment at Derna had an important airport in its area and could provide a useful halfway house should there be an outbreak of hostilities in Egypt which might threaten British citizens or possibly an invasion of Cyrenaica. King Idris I was on a somewhat unstable throne as he had been established by the British after the defeat of the Italians in the War. There was a British Resident in the country stationed at Benghazi and he acted as the eyes and ears of the British Foreign Office. Although the King was head of the Senussi tribe when he was appointed, his control of the country was somewhat slight and he hadn't been on the throne very long. Altogether it seemed the domestic scene was one of some instability and the Regiment was part of a full army division which had been stationed in the country as part of the terms of the British settlement. The British, therefore, had a mandate not dissimilar to the kind of mandate that they had at one point in the development of Palestine.

John Burton and I then drove in somewhat stately fashion in the Colonel's Humber car 200 miles up the road to Derna. This was a very pretty place with plenty of shade under the palm trees and not so much heat because of the offshore breeze. Our barracks, however, were pretty small as was only fitting for the detachment of one squadron under our Officer Commanding, Major Fletcher, who was almost as new to the regiment as we were. Nevertheless, he seemed an agreeable person although we were soon to discover that he was liable to panic or at least that's what it looked like!

The Second Lieutenant's role is not a mighty one, unless in times of conflict. It is mainly concerned with maintaining a state of readiness, particularly amongst the vehicles in his command and maintaining a high degree of enthusiasm amongst the troops who far too often were bored stiff. As a troop leader I was allocated B Troop which consisted of four armoured cars each with a crew of three, driver, commander and wireless operator. It should be added that these armoured cars, left over from the War, were manufactured originally by Daimler and had seen a substantial amount of service. There was plenty of maintenance to be done to keep them in good order, the joints of the transmission kept leaking, engines quite frequently boiled over, but above all the guns were considered somewhat unsafe and only fired on ranges with very great care. One or two had exploded from shells caught inside and as the Sergeant said, 'The barrel's peeled back like a bloody banana.' I decided to give each armoured car a name and settled on English admirals. This had somewhat quaint results as they all had to have the initial letter B. As there was not a great field of choice we ended up with a peculiar bunch of names which were Byng, Boscawen, Beattie and Benbow. It was pointed out that Admiral Byng was one of the Navy's mighty failures who lost the island of Minorca to the French and was promptly shot on his quarterdeck 'pour encourager les autres', as Voltaire said.

The matter of naming the vehicles was not as great a problem as a second slightly more important one. The moment I got into my car I discovered that I could not stand on the floor of the car and see out of the top. Corporal Thompson immediately went off to find some box or equivalent which would allow me to stand on to see out of the top. He went to the cookhouse for this and came back very shortly with a tin of dehydrated cabbage as issued by the War Office for soldiers in all parts of the world. This was empty and thus free to be used for alternative purposes. It fitted perfectly on the floor and provided me with the height necessary for the head and shoulders to look out of the vehicle. He rapidly scratched the words 'Sir's tin' on it and it became a vital part of my equipment for my role as troop leader. Whenever I visited other vehicles I had to take the tin with me and, of course, it fitted perfectly wherever I went. You can imagine how

Standing on 'Sir's' tin, National Service, Tripoli, 1951.

Sir's Tin.

important I found Corporal Thompson in dealing with the solution of major problems.

There was plenty of slack time on station in Derna and despite the best that John Burton and I could think of we found it difficult to keep the men all happily engaged. Sports activity loomed large, but for the relatively slender numbers at our disposal it wasn't easy to raise teams for anything except football. We did, however, go some way to raise a team suitable for cross-country running because there was a divisional sports event which included that particular skill. And then there was a special cross-country affair for which I got summoned back to Barce. Apparently the entire division was to have a sports day which was to include a cross-country run of some 7 or 8 miles and the Army was invited to supply teams on a regimental level. One of the 'regiments' that had been invited was the King's Bodyguard which consisted of extremely tall and lithe Nubians whose reputation in running cross country in desert conditions was simply fantastic. I was asked to get up a team to do some training and to get fell in to go and win that event. We did our level best, but frankly I didn't feel we had a single chance of getting anywhere near those Nubians. We travelled to the stadium at Benghazi although the race was to be run across country and therefore we left the stadium fairly quickly. Sure enough the race was led by a chap on a white horse which shot off as soon as the starter's pistol had fired and off we trundled out of the stadium and up the road and on to the flat land surrounding Benghazi. The chap on the white horse was quickly reduced to a plume of sand and there followed after him seven of these amazing Nubians, the blackest and probably the shiniest you could find, with the savour of body lotion wafting in the heat. We came nowhere near winning this event but I think it should be put on record that I was the first white man home. The King's guard took the first seven places. I suspect if they hadn't they might have been shot in the morning.

And then suddenly the day dawned when we started to get orders from headquarters in Barce that the Regiment had to equip itself for a military event in support of a war emergency. The emergency took the form of a possible revolt in Cairo which if it spread to Alexandria might threaten the livelihood and properties of British citizens. This was the beginning of the challenge to King Farouk by General Neguib which had been fermenting for some time. The British were proposing to form a major force to frighten the Egyptians, and to demonstrate our determination to move in to rescue our citizens if that were needed. The 16th/5th Lancers had to move in wartime order to the Egyptian frontier near Tobruk. As B Squadron were already stationed halfway there we were the natural ones to lead this expedition. When we got our orders we had already been made aware that the RAF were reinforcing their garrison at Derna airport, and we were told that a Naval force would also be assembled in Tobruk harbour for the purpose of evacuation. It turned out to be two cruisers and the aircraft carrier *Bulwark* with a destroyer in waiting. The Army was to be reinforced by the arrival of a Guards detachment together with the First Battalion Highland Light Infantry. News sped round B Squadron like wildfire and we all realised that our hour of destiny had come The first slight snag in the proceedings was when we were issued with our two-pounder ammunition. It was so old it had to be stored lashed to the *outside* of the vehicle.

The order about ammunition caused me considerable concern. If the ammunition was to be carried on the outside of the vehicle it seemed to me very likely that a loose rifle shot from the enemy might blow up a box of it and the car as well; and if the ammunition was of such delicate proportions that it had to be handled in this way it didn't sound to me as though it was going to be much good. However, orders were orders and we strapped boxes of ammunition around each of the cars with some difficulty.

When we reached the outskirts of Tobruk and arrived where we were going to laager up for the night we lifted off the ammunition with some delicacy. Sergeant Thompson's car had placed the boxes some distance from the armoured car but during manoeuvres to park the vehicle Taffy Enoch, his reliable driver from Wales, could not see clearly behind him and he actually reversed and ran over a box of the ammunition. There was general panic as people threw themselves to the floor but Enoch's 7-ton armoured car rolled gently over the box squashing it almost completely and the shells inside.

Not to be outperformed by anyone Enoch then put his vehicle into forward gear and rolled forward ensuring that his 7 tons once again went over the same box of ammunition. Absolutely no explosion, not even a fart! B Squadron had managed to prove that the ammunition was useless. This information was conveyed to higher authority who came to have a look and agreed with our diagnosis. I think someone from the Ordnance Regiment was summoned to take it all away and as far as my memory goes I don't think we were issued with any other two-pounder ammunition on the not unreasonable grounds that it was likely to be of the same age as the one which had already proved useless. However, we did have ammunition for Bren guns which were mounted co-axially with the two-pounder and it was reckoned that if there were riots the Bren gun was probably just as good if not better. Needless to say Taffy Enoch was elected a hero amongst the lads for his unflinching devotion to duty and for not having abandoned his car during the process of manoeuvring.

Whilst we may not have engaged in live ammunition shooting, the armoured cars were used for escort duty from the El Adem airport which was run of course by the RAF and into Tobruk town. The Navy had already arrived in the bay in some strength and we applied escort duties to the field commanders of the HLI and the Third Grenadiers. This involved making our vehicles extremely smart, washed and polished throughout and with the 16th/5th pennons flying from the wireless aerials. We had the Humber staff car in which the colonels travelled but they had one of my 7-tonners running in front and one behind to give them the feeling of proper cavalry treatment.

As the Egyptians didn't riot and all appeared to be peaceful in Alexandria the state of readiness was reduced and we were on stand-by but not immediate readiness to move. This allowed some sporting fixtures to be arranged between different regiments and we were also able to take part in parties which the Navy decided to throw. I thus found myself spending my twentieth birthday at a splendid party on board the cruiser *Sheffield*. Amazingly there was a Commander Sheffield on board this ship and he was about my size if not slightly smaller. I well remember arriving at the ship and making my way gingerly up the rope ladder to the deck but I am damned if I can remember leaving the ship; I doubt if I could have done it without assistance. Before we took the road home there was another little episode which requires recording.

We took the troop out for a little run in the desert between Tobruk and the town of Sidi Rezegh and flushed out a small flock of great bustards, a fine wild turkey of a bird which is found in very large numbers wintering in desert country. I gave the order to Lance Corporal Thacker to charge after the flock of birds and he went off like a rocket. We were happily engaged in this chase when I noticed there appeared to be a lot of molehills around so I called up Corporal Thompson to ask him what he thought they were. He came back with the information 'I rather think they are mines, sir.' That sounded a much more likely explanation than moles who would have to be pretty red hot to survive in this sort of country and the lines were fairly regular when one came to look at them. I ordered Thacker to stop and we had a consultation.

One of the great virtues of the Daimler armoured car is that it's rear engined and it also has a steering wheel located under the commander's seat for use if it is required to reverse at speed because it could go backwards as fast as it could go forwards. I undertook to take this reverse steering wheel, look through the slits and try to keep within the very clear marks of the wheels of the Daimler which Thacker had already made on the way in to this problem. Needless to say, we reversed very slowly and after about ten minutes we cleared the minefield, much to the relief of Corporal Thacker who although he couldn't steer the way backwards and couldn't see at all where he was going felt he had been responsible for getting us into this fix. The answer was that I was responsible for it because I shouldn't go chasing bustards in His Majesty's armoured cars!

The minefields in the desert were systematically cleared, not by the British Army or indeed by the Germany Army who probably laid them, but by the nomadic Arabs because they themselves had established a fairly lucrative industry of blowing up the wrecked tanks and other military hardware that the German and Italian armies had left behind with the mines. They then collected all the small pieces of metal from their explosions, strapped them on to lorries that they had probably rescued from the same fate and took them down to the various ports of Benghazi or Tobruk where they were shipped across to Italy and melted down for re-use. Frequently one would hear explosions going on to remind us all that the minefields were being systematically cleared.

One of the other sights around the desert were the little shrines which the Arabs erected to mark their dead. These are nearly always painted white and can be seen from a long way off. They were very small buildings and we stopped at one and were having a look inside when I noted that Corporal Thacker did not appear from within his car. I asked him why and he replied in his broad Doncaster accent, 'Ahm not ganging in there, thee 'as to tek thee biats off', and he had strong views about that.

It was during 1951 that the 16th/5th were converted from armoured cars to Comet tanks and it also moved from Barce across to Sabratha near Tripoli where the 4th/7th Dragoon Guards were leaving their tanks on being posted back to UK. The handing in of the armoured cars was a sad occasion even though they had not shown themselves wholly efficient. They were a fun vehicle and we thought that we would mark the occasion by having a race amongst the vehicles across the desert. This very nearly turned into disaster as one of the vehicles hit a sudden soft patch in the sand, and spun round nearly turning over. That would certainly have killed the commander and it would have caused a major court of inquiry to be held. As one of those participating, my short life as an officer and a gentleman would have come to a shuddering end. It also meant goodbye to 'Sir's tin' of dehydrated cabbage as the Comet tank allowed me more space and a seat to stand on which allowed me to see out of the top perfectly well. The tanks were not friendly things, being big and noisy and we all had to learn how to drive them and how to manoeuvre them because they worked on the principle of a brake on each side locking onto the track and thus spinning the vehicle from left to right by skidding it. It played havoc on any road surface but was perfectly acceptable in the desert. The Comets were fast little tanks and a very substantial improvement on the heavy and slow models with which the Army had been equipped hitherto.

The Regiment also changed its Colonel in 1951 when Colonel Douglas Kaye went out and Colonel Jock Cleghorn took his place. Colonel Jock was a much more fiery individual than Colonel Douglas and we subalterns felt that things might get a little bit stroppy. Indeed they did. The first such occasion occurred on the day that had been designated a practice day for regimental sport and most of us were engaged with our various teams in doing just that. But my very good friend John Burton felt this was a waste of his talents; in any case he didn't hold much to sports. So he slid off for a quiet kip dressed in those famous underpants known throughout the Army as drawers. I noticed the approaching Colonel coming towards me as he was clearly looking for something or someone. When he asked if I had seen John Burton I replied, 'I am sure he is fully engaged in practising with his men, sir.' Cleghorn didn't regard this as a satisfactory answer and stormed his way to the Officers' Mess where he went round all the rooms and discovered Burton stretched out, fast asleep in his underpants. With a roar of 'Burton what do you think you are doing?' John was quickly roused and told to come to the Colonel's office in the morning. From that day to this John Burton was always known at Kipper Burton. Happily Colonel Jock had cooled down a bit by the morning and Burton was given some tasks to do which had to be done immediately and accurately.

The whole Regiment was now together again and this allowed the regimental band to play at guest nights in the Officers' Mess when we wore No. 1 dress and had the regimental silverware out on display. The band was a splendid diversion and the Regiment was very proud of the way in which they used to win inter-regimental contests and by performing in many places raised much-needed money to support it. When senior or junior officers left the Regiment to return to UK they were dined out in style, including being able to choose the music to be played on such an occasion. Colonels from other regiments came, the local administrator came and we began to widen our circle of acquaintanceship.

Guest nights did have another aspect which was the horseplay in the early hours of the morning when whisky took its toll. This was something of a hazardous enterprise for the smallest officer on board. I recall being thrown from one end of the Officers' Mess to the other on the assumption that I would be caught in the safe hands of one of the other officers, a considerable risk because the effects of whisky were more or less universal. However, I survived this at least once and got pensioned off this particular privilege as my seniority increased. The occasional guest night in the Sergeants' Mess was a different matter altogether. The Regimental Sergeant Major and the Sergeant quartermaster were splendidly big soldiers and there was much mirth and no risk in their tossing me from one to the other. My main role in the Sergeants' Mess parties however was to recite little ditties like Stanley Holloway's monologues, 'The Battle of Hastings' and 'Magna Carta', followed by a song which I wrote with Captain Michael Codrington, the Second in Command of the Squadron, based upon the refrain 'Ring the bell Sexton, ring the bell ring'. This included verses about many of those who had participated in the big drive up to Tobruk when the Squadron set out on its false alarm to rescue the Brits of Alexandria. As this referred obliquely to all the characters in the Sergeants' Mess and many of the officers including the Commanding Officer it scored a substantial success and was repeated *ad nauseam* when these functions took place. The only verse to survive was the verse on Captain Hall, who was immensely smooth and always immaculately turned out:

> Caviar in wicker box,
> Golden cufflinks – purple socks,
> Perspex mapboard – maps galore,
> Captain Hall is going to war!

The 16th Lancers were raised in Ireland in the days of George III, and his wife Queen Caroline was the patron of the Regiment, her cipher being used by the Regiment on all its military buttons. It was a unit which became part of the English army whereas the 5th Lancers, again raised in Ireland, are a distinctly Irish regiment, so Irish in fact that they mutinied in their barracks at the Curragh near Dublin during the First World War. This caused such a fuss that they were disbanded and allied with the 16th to become the most junior cavalry regiment in the Army. However, eventually all was forgiven and the best way of demonstrating this was the agreement that Princess Elizabeth as she then was should become the Honorary Colonel-in-Chief of this particular regiment. As it turned out this was a mightily important decision because in February 1952 King George VI died. This was marked by a major memorial service held in the barracks at Sabratha. Armbands were worn by all officers for about a week and it was recognised that there was a possibility that Princess Elizabeth, now Her Majesty Queen Elizabeth II, might allow her contact with the regiment to be continued. In due time we heard that this honour had indeed been continued and the Queen was, therefore, the Colonel-in-Chief of the 16th/5th Lancers. Eventually, due to reductions in the Services, the 16th/5th was again merged with another old cavalry regiment, namely the 17th/21st. By that time the 16th/5th was known as the Queen's Royal Lancers and that name was used for the merged unit. So the history of the Regiment more or less ran full circle – it was started by a Queen of England and it was eventually merged by a Queen of England in the 1990s.

The year 1952 did, however, bring the prospect of university education nearer and the conclusion of our National Service nearer too. Several of us had earnest conversations about whether we might continue in the Army as professional soldiers because it was quite clear we had enjoyed our time, that we had learned a lot and could carry out the role of junior officers with considerably more confidence than we had at the outset.

Again the Army brings great companionship, particularly in small regiments like ours and we would be losing very good friends if we were to leave in time to go up to university in October. Frankly all of those who had obtained places at university felt it would be wrong to throw that element of our education away, simply because we had enjoyed our military service which had been an obligation rather than a choice. So John Burton and I were dined out by the Regiment in great style with the band on peak performance with a medley from Gilbert and Sullivan, including the First Sea Lord's song and we hitched a lift on an RAF plane from Tripoli airport which brought us back to the UK early in September.

The time had come to launch ourselves onto the barrack square at Cambridge with a view to completing our education with some of the military precision we had learned during our army service.

I should add at this point that the College's policy on rooms was to provide accommodation within the College for all first-year students. The second year would be out in lodgings in the town and the third year would probably be back in College sharing with some other colleague. For reasons which should not be too closely examined, in our second year Peter Wordie and I shared rooms which had been specially selected to have a wonderful riverside view over the Bridge of Sighs and its attendant boating and punting traffic. Although buns could occasionally be thrown at chums in punts such missiles were frowned upon and we had to do it in great secrecy. I also became a member of the May Ball Committee feeling it might justify a free ticket or two. St John's held a May Ball at the end of each summer term and it was an event which was very costly but nevertheless was well supported. The Ball also had a major feast within it – by tradition St John's had the right by Royal dispensation to serve cold roast swan at these proceedings.

In our second year too we joined the Lady Margaret Boat Club so that we could take part in the Lent bumps. The LMBC was a very large boat club and raised seven or eight boats for the main events in the Lent term and of course in the summer term. I coxed the 7th Gentleman's boat and quite enjoyed it, although in the bump races it is a rather difficult job. You not only have to keep the boat straight but you also have to chase as fast as you can to hit the boat in front. The weather was pretty cold and the cox was colder than most but luck was with us and we did secure a bump. I have to admit that it was somewhat odd because quite frankly Fitzwilliam 3, which was in front of us, stopped rowing for some extraordinary reason and as I couldn't avoid it we went bonk into the stern, thus securing the only bump for the Lady Margaret Boat Club in the entire Lent races. We, therefore, made our mark in this fascinating sport and I have a photograph proudly in my study to record the fact.

It was in this second year also that girls became an important feature of our lives. Cambridge was blessed with three colleges in which girls resided. The days of cohabitation in colleges had not yet begun though they were fast approaching. The girls in college at New Hall had just started and I think contained twelve at the commencement of the Lent term. Girton and Newnham however were full of bubbling beauties. In the history faculty we found the irrepressible Julia Boulton. Because of her rich red hair she was nicknamed 'Coppernob' by us all and was the life and soul of any party you might invite her to or any that you were lucky enough to go to yourself. She was, I might add, relatively short which I found a huge asset but her voice could be heard 5 miles downwind on a cold and frosty morning as she bicycled her way down from Girton to the history lecture halls. Coppernob was the first girl to whom I was indebted when she accepted a visit to my rooms in First Court to take a cup of afternoon tea. Later in more affluent times we introduced sherry wine and ultimately gin which I suspect was her favourite tipple. She was great company and much beloved by many men.

Then there was Moira Hamilton also from the history faculty. Compared to Julia she was calm and patience personified, a lovely girl to whom I was very much attracted. When we moved rooms into New Court and had our large suite overlooking the Bridge of Sighs she was a regular visitor. I found that standing on a little step in the bay window I was exactly her height and this led to much adoration and kissing of lips. She ultimately went for higher stakes and married one of the hockey blues and went out to live, I believe, in Australia. The whole United Kingdom grieved for her loss and copious tears were shed.

Ian and I took Moira and his friend Judy Beck to the Gilbert and Sullivan operas produced at the Arts Theatre in Cambridge. The first one we saw was *Princess Ida* which is rarely performed and played to full houses, fully justified by the quality of the production. It was also during the Lent term that I was arraigned before the Magistrates of the City of Cambridge. As usual dashing down to the river when we were already late I rode my bicycle over a footbridge and virtually fell into the arms of the law. I was charged with driving a bicycle without due care and attention and was fined £5, a not inconsiderable sum. When the Magistrate asked me if I had anything to say I said, 'Yes, sir. I have never seen that policeman who gave evidence in my life before.' A titter went round the court as the prosecution explained that the policeman in question had only recently grown his smart moustache. Nevertheless, my plea was dismissed and £5 duly paid.

The Lent term was also a time for feasting and the Caledonian Club duly had its Burns' Night Dinner which P.J. Wordie in full Scots regalia went off to attend. He returned in the early hours of the morning and miraculously found his way into our rooms, but such was his condition that he was unable to find the bedroom door, so after attacking the corner vigorously he fell in a heap from which I was unable to recover him until after breakfast the next morning. His enthusiasm for all things Caledonian was in no sense diminished. I became keen on the Union Society and attended most of the debates which were presided over by President Alistair Sampson who had one of the strongest wits in the University. According to tradition the first debate of the term was one of no confidence in Her Majesty's Government, proposed on behalf of the Conservative Opposition by Iain Macleod, and opposed by the Rt Hon Herbert Morrison who was at that time Foreign Secretary. It was an eloquent occasion with Iain Macleod taking the main honours with this following extract:

> If there were to be a race tomorrow between all those who had mishandled, and I use that word deliberately, the foreign affairs of this state, I predict that Lord North would come first and that there would be a deadheat for second place between the Rt Hon Gentleman and Ethelred.

When President Sampson had his Presidential Debate he included the following: 'The other day to my surprise my uncle left me twelve glass eyes. He never used these things himself but kept them all upon a shelf and champing on the shelf beneath were twenty-seven sets of teeth.'

I set out to become President of the Union, accepted invitations to other College debating societies like the Mildmay Essay Club at Christ's College and also proposed toasts at many good dinners in aid of many good causes, one of them being to become known in other colleges as a likely Union performer.

I made my maiden speech in a debate starring Hermione Gingold, beginning my contribution by referring to her as Mrs Gin Gold which amused the troops and I then produced the following ditty:

Miss Walrus and Miss Carpenter.

Miss Walrus and Miss Carpenter were walking hand in hand
And musing on the miseries of being undermanned
If only undergraduates, they said, would understand
'If seven beauty-treatment girls attacked my pimply face
Do you suppose,' Miss Walrus said, 'they'd give me charm and grace?'
'I doubt it,' said Miss Carpenter and quickened up the pace.
'You have not got the gifts, my dear, of carriage, ease and poise.
For plaits, bowlegs and spectacles do not appeal to boys.'
'I know I lack,' Miss Walrus said, 'some of the earthly joys
But you yourself are angular, thick-lipped, flat-nosed and stout,
And would seem to me more shapely if you turned yourself about.'
'I know it,' said Miss Carpenter, 'there is no need to shout.'
They walked back to their Colleges growing steadily morose
Discussing how much arsenic would make a lethal dose
And why old spinsters go berserk, and veins go varicose . . .

The second extract from Union speeches is dated 1954, is entitled
'Mr Kipling' and hears that a lot of Southern Railway crockery was
recently deliberately smashed because it bore the telltale insignia of
private ownership:

'Tell me Daddy, is it true that you fought at Waterloo
Midst all the din of battle and the blood,
Saw soldiers fall and die and turned a sickly eye
As horses trampled guardsmen in the mud?'

'No, sonny, Waterloo is a station just like Crewe,
Though the noise was something shocking, I recall,
With all the sounds of battle, the crashing and the rattle
As we bunged them "S.R." teacups at the wall.'

Boots, boots, boots, boots crunching up and down again
Crushing charlie chinaware beneath the workers' heel
For too long they've been getting at the bleeding proletariat
The boot's now on the other foot – Hurrah for Fortune's wheel!

'Now Sonny, when you read of this happy happy breed
That forms the British Empire's population
Just call to mind the fight 'gainst capitalism's blight
Which resulted in our blessed emancipation.

For now the country's run by nearly everyone,
No longer only them's as 'unts and shoots,
And thank your lucky star for the good old NUR,
Three cheers for them's as only shunts and hoots!'

Puff, puff, puff, puff goes the steaming railway train
The symbol of democracy and progress, wrought in steel.
For the hearts are in the boots of the blokes as 'unts and shoots
They've met their final Waterloo – Hurrah for Fortune's wheel!

It is a fact that my regular appearance at the Union aided and abetted my passage towards office. The fact is that there were only three elected officers, the President, Vice-President and the Secretary and a standing committee of six members which was also a usual stepping-off point. If you wished to succeed to the Presidency you had really to be holding the secretary's place so that your chances of being Vice-President in the term afterwards were secured and if you secured the Vice-Presidency then it was almost inevitable that you become President the following term.

So it was I became Secretary in the Michaelmas term of 1953 when Hugh Thomas was President, became Vice-President in the Easter term of 1953 when Nicholas Tomalin was President, and succeeded him as President, being elected unopposed for the Michaelmas term in 1954. The elections being held at the end of the preceding term I then had the whole of the long vacation available to plan and hopefully execute a good range of debates and activities which might stimulate membership of the Union at the beginning of that Michaelmas term.

Initially, I had a slice of luck. The Clerk to the Union Society, one Sidney Elwood, came to me during the vacation with an important message from the Ethiopian Embassy. This indicated that the Emperor Haile Selasse, known as the Lion of Judah, was going to make a state visit to this country and a letter duly winged its way to the Embassy inviting His Imperial Majesty to come and visit the Cambridge Union which had conferred honorary membership upon the Emperor when he visited this country last in 1936 during the war with Italy over Abyssinia and Ethiopia. The struggle of the Ethiopians against the Italians who used gas was a pitiful spectacle which roused indignation worldwide, particularly in this country and particularly also in Cambridge. During that time a banner suddenly appeared one morning stretched between two pinnacles on the roof of King's College Chapel. The banner read simply 'Save Ethiopia'. The Provost of King's summoned his College Dons together to discover how that banner had been erected between those two pinnacles at an inaccessible portion of the College Chapel roof. The Dons were very reticent about this and indeed nobody volunteered until suddenly the most distinguished Don of all, namely Maynard Keynes, the great and celebrated economist, admitted that he had done it. How had he done it? asked the Provost. 'You may not realise just how skilful I am at rock climbing,' he replied, 'but if you would kindly forget the episode I will take it down for you.' Against this background the suggestion that the Union should honour the Emperor was a good one and His Imperial Majesty agreed to come. This produced a coup which would be a singularly unusual star in the Union programme for the Michaelmas term. I thought this would also increase the numbers wishing to join the Union. So this particular spectacle was worked into the programme with the greatest alacrity. Sadly, like so many union events, in the end through sheer frustration, it was taken out of His Imperial Majesty's programme by the FCO.

However, nothing daunted we decided to do something much less spectacular but nonetheless quite original. We decided to hold a Union Ball, the first ever, in the debating chamber, having checked that we could actually move out all the furniture and get in a dance floor and include a suitable orchestra. The Union Ball, therefore, was the highlight of the Michaelmas term as far as drumming up support for the Union Society was concerned. Hardly a debating occasion, but nonetheless an event which would attract a lot of people. We then set to work putting into place a programme of orthodox debates which would be up to the usual Cambridge standard but perhaps just a little beyond it.

After the end of the summer term the President for the Michaelmas term began working hard to try and assemble a range of debating topics and a range of speakers who would fulfil the

Cambridge Union Society 1954.

Back row, left to right: R.J. O'Neill, Trinity; E.A.V. Ebsworth, King's; J.N. Crichton-Miller, Pembroke; R.G. Moore, Trinity; J.G. York, Clare; I. Harland, Peterhouse; A.R. Watkins, Queens'. Front row, left to right: J.D. Waite, Corpus Christi, Secretary; R. Weinberg, Ex-President Yale Political Union; M. Heseltine, President Oxford Union; J.G.D. Shaw, St. John's, President; Miss Jennifer Copeman, President University of London Union; G. Parker, President Glasgow Union Society; T. Dalyell, King's, Vice President.

presidential requirement of getting a lot of people to attend debates, allowing a range of topics to be discussed which would stimulate the attendance of a significant audience. The precursor to this was to establish a very vigorous campaign of recruitment at the commencement of the Michaelmas term amongst the freshmen to the university. I hoped they would find the Union an attractive place to join and come and assist in the debates, and thus commence a career of supporting the Union which might well lead to the officers and presidents of the future. This was undertaken by the President and his chief officers, the Vice-Presidents, Secretary and members of the committee who went round the colleges at the commencement of the new term and held what were known as 'squashes', which provided a meeting place in the College where officers could talk to them about the Union and its activities and recruit members, hopefully on a lifetime basis which thus became the bedrock of income into the Union funds. The President's objective would be to try and get somewhere near 700 new members so that the Union could continue in existence and provide the University with a range of topics which they would regard as both interesting and appropriate for discussion. Typical of these debates was the debate of No Confidence in HM Government which was the traditional topic for the commencement of the Michaelmas term. We were fortunate in having a success at recruitment. This provided something between 650 and 700 new members which did indeed provide not only large numbers at attendance but also a large number of people to vote on the decisions taken at the end of the debate which demonstrated the University's feeling on these topics.

The first debate on 12th October was on the motion that 'Her Majesty's Government is no longer deserving of the confidence of this house'. It was proposed by Richard Moore who was the leading Liberal in the Union and was opposed by Mr Tam Dalyell who in those days was not Chairman of the Labour Party but in fact Chairman of the Conservative Party of the University. The main speaker in favour of the motion was the Rt Hon Geoffrey Lloyd, a past President of the Union who was currently in office as Minister for Fuel and Power. Interestingly enough Mr Hugh Gaitskell spoke for the Labour Government and was the actual Minister for Fuel and Power at this time. The debate drew a number of speakers including Mr Samuel Brittan who became a very staunch Labour economist and a very wise man indeed. He is the elder brother of Leon Brittan who became Home Secretary and Minister for Industry in Margaret Thatcher's government and subsequently Vice-President of the Commission on the European stage. The speeches were all of a high order and there was a very substantial vote. In the division 273 supported the motion but 500 voted against it being a majority of 227 against the government of the day.

There then followed a debate about the separation of the Church and state being essential to the future of Christianity. This was a somewhat esoteric subject but nevertheless 520 people attended and the vote was a narrow one; 262 voting in favour of separation of Church and state, and 288, a majority of only 26, voting against it. Then there was a debate about the role of the independent schools in the education system. This was proposed by Mr Neil Crichton-Miller, a Conservative whose father at that time was the Headmaster of Stowe School. It was won in the division by 261 votes in favour with 111 against, being a sizeable majority of 150 for the maintenance of the independent sector.

There followed a debate on the humorous topic, namely 'This House deplores the disappearance of the chaperone'. This debate was famous for one omission and one inclusion. We were due to have the irrepressible Lady Isobel Barnet as the main speaker in favour of this proposition, but she unfortunately had to cancel very late. She was a great favourite of the TV screen with the panel game *What's My Line?*. I was extremely stranded in this matter because she had attracted a large audience which included my mother and father because they were both extremely keen on Lady Isobel and wanted to have the opportunity of hearing her at first hand. My mother, however, was not without considerable resource when it came to speaking in public and I prevailed upon her to take Lady Barnet's place at the eleventh hour and provide a double first, namely that the President had invited his mother to speak at the Cambridge Union, and this was the first time that she had ever addressed an assembly of this kind. She therefore appeared on the order paper as Alderman Mrs Shaw JP and I was able to summon her from the Chair by saying I now call upon my Mum to address the assembly. She spoke impromptu for about five minutes and had a rousing ovation when she sat down. I came down from the Chair and gave her a big kiss and presented her with the carnation from my buttonhole to rapturous applause. The vote in question was 385 in favour of the motion and 277 against. A very substantial turnout indeed.

There were other debates on the trade unions, the fall of the House of Stuart – a somewhat melancholy subject – and a debate on National Service being both inopportune and inexpedient, which was lost by a margin of 38 votes somewhat to my surprise. There was also a vote on the motion that 'This House prefers subjection to Communism to the consequences of a Third World War' which provided a majority for the motion of 9 votes, a rather shattering result. I think the outcome was profoundly influenced by Sam Brittan making a stirring speech in favour. As a matter of interest the BBC selected this for broadcasting the following night.

So the Union got into full swing on topics which were of relevance although the vein of wit, and satire, which was a feature of Cambridge debates at that time, was also firmly in evidence. The debate on Trade Unions was enlivened by two contributions of real merit. One was the contribution of Miss Alice Bacon who was the Labour Minister for Education and in the same debate a contribution from Mr J. Enoch Powell MP, a man who at that time was at the height of his powers. The debate on Church and State was also enlivened by a contribution by Dr Martin Niemoller who had single-handedly made such a stand against Hitler in Germany to seek to protect the Christian religion and the role of the Churches in that beleaguered state. The Bishop of Southwell also spoke in favour of maintaining the *status quo*. He had come to the notice of the University, not only because his daughter Rosemary was at Girton and a very good friend of ours, but also because he delivered a quite amazing sermon in the University Church of Great St Mary's in the summer term. We all filed in to support Rosemary though we got rather confused when the Bishop rose to the pulpit in Great St

Mary's, one hymn too soon in the Order of Service. Being a brave man he ran it strongly by saying, 'Sorry, I'll go down and we'll start that again.' He returned to the pulpit at the appropriate time and we all remember to this day his opening words which were as follows:

> I'm glad to see you all here today filling this mighty church and demonstrating your commitment to this university to which you have all come with your own brains and somebody else's income tax. What are you all going to do in the years ahead? I was told by one of my clergy the other day who had attended the Parish Garden Fete that he asked a young boy of about 11 'Sonny, what are you going to be when you grow up?' The boy replied, 'A sex maniac'. Well, you know, it takes all sorts to make a world.

Needless to say there was a thumping good collection from this splendid contribution. So I ensured that he came to the Union to speak on a matter of greater importance and we were not disappointed.

In addition to these debates the President had to attend a number of special functions at which debates took place outside Cambridge. I made a point of going to as many of the 'red brick' universities as possible to strengthen the links between the old and the new. I was also invited to a very special occasion which was the celebratory dinner marking the 100th anniversary foundation of the University of London. This took the form of a dinner and dance, the dinner presided over by the Chancellor of the University, HRH The Princess Alice of Athlone. I had no doubt that I wished to be accompanied by someone worthy of the occasion, and so it was that I invited the illustrious Coppernob herself, Julia Boulton, to fulfil that task. And I have to say that she fulfilled it admirably. It has to be said that we were a little late arriving at the Senate House and I was somewhat sorry to note that the participants had already gone in to take their places for the dinner. I mentioned to Julia that we would have to make a late entry and I looked forward to the best curtsy she could manage to HRH and the Vice Chancellor. Julia was in a marvellous jet-black dress with a jewel appended at the shoulder and she looked a million dollars with red hair flashing in the spotlights.

We were duly announced by the flunkey at the gate and swept in and walked the considerable distance to the high table where our places were ominously displayed. I gave Julia a twirl and she made a magnificent curtsy down to the deck and duly kissed the Princess's hand in her velvet glove. About fifteen minutes later the doors opened and the President of Oxford was announced. In came Mr Michael Heseltine. I have to say he was in his early mode, very tall, very blonde and somewhat Prussian in appearance. Needless to say he had a fantastic blonde on his arm, but her curtsy was not a patch on Julia's and I think Cambridge won firmly on points in this first encounter. I also met Michael Heseltine when we debated at Lloyds of London in their fabulous library. I can't remember much of the debate but I can remember being taken away afterwards to the Savoy where in the private room (the Pinafore Room) we had a fabulous dinner provided by one of the affluent members of that great institution. I was introduced to Port Salut cheese on that occasion, a memory which still lingers.

We came to the Union Ball and I have to say that although I shouldn't, it was a fabulous success. Here again Julia was my partner and that dress once again swept the occasion. My brother and his wife came down and we had a sell-out which provided not only a first-class evening but also a substantial contribution to Union funds. I noted that Mr Michael Heseltine subsequently opened a nightclub in both cellars of the Union at Oxford and invited the rich but vulgar Lady Docker to formally open the nightclub. Ah, well, it does indeed take all sorts to make a world.

The final debate of the term when the President chooses his own topic and hands over to the incoming President was also a rather special occasion. I invited the Presidents of Unions of various provincial universities to come and speak on that date. So we had not only Jennifer Copeman, the President from London, but also Presidents from Queen's Belfast, Glasgow University and the University College Bangor to represent the various parts of the United Kingdom. The motion for debate? 'The English, like all good dogs, have had their day'. This was a motion for nostalgia for the great Imperial past and also an opportunity for much mirth and wit at the expense of ourselves who, after all, are best placed to take a nostalgic view of our own history. It was a glorious occasion and I was received with a standing ovation from my Union members.

Michael Heseltine spoke and spoke well and then muttered to me during the ovation, 'You will never ever receive an ovation like this again.' I suspect he was right. Incidentally, the tradition that Oxford would come to speak at Cambridge and Cambridge would come to speak at Oxford was rather tactlessly broken when it came to Michael Heseltine's Presidential debate. I received two tickets for the Strangers' Gallery. Ah well, it takes all sorts to make a world.

Before closing this chapter on the Presidency of the Union in Michaelmas 1954, three other matters should be dealt with. First my successor was not my Vice-President Tam Dalyell nor my Secretary John Waite, it was in fact Mr Richard Moore of Trinity College who had been Secretary in the Easter term of 1954. He decided to oppose Tam Dalyell for the Presidency and in a needle election he won over the incumbent Vice-President, a most unusual affair and one that should be noted. There was an element of political activity here because Richard was a strong Liberal whereas Tam Dalyell was Chairman of the Conservative Association in the University. I have to remind the reader that electioneering in the form of canvassing was not permitted under Union rules and when such an outbreak occurred there were inquiries by one of the senior officers and disciplines were applied. But it was a very severe blow to Tam who during the next few months came under the influence of his supervisor at King's, Noel Annan and ultimately decided to switch from Conservative to Socialist. In that regard he fought and won a needle by-election in Linlithgow, supported by the National Union of Scottish Mineworkers, against a Scottish National candidate, Mr Wolfe. From then on his political career on the national stage was clearly established and he became in time one of the most experienced of Parliamentarians.

The second point to make was that in January of 1955 the Union was invited to submit two names to go on a debating tour of the universities in eastern Canada. I opted for myself (there was little choice) and I took with me J.D. Waite of Corpus Christi College who had been Secretary during the last Michaelmas term. The tour was arranged by the British Council and we had the most wonderful time despite the fact that it all took place in January which was not the best month for travel to Canada. It was marked by many instances, not least of which was when the aeroplane on which John Waite and I were travelling out to Montreal was delayed after two of the engines caught fire over the North Atlantic and it was deemed necessary to turn back to Prestwick for repairs and maintenance. This enabled us to be accommodated in the Turnberry Hotel on the coast of Ayrshire at the liberal expense of BOAC. As a result of this we lost one day of our tour itinerary but we had a very jolly time notwithstanding.

The third point to make is that having achieved the Presidency of the Union I found myself in some demand for radio or television interviews as a leading representative of the University, and I was also invited to attend a number of events and speak on a number of issues. Amongst these were the insurance debating society of London, Newcastle University Union, the University of London Union where we were televised and other local fora. The Vice-President's report for the term, which is an official document now housed in the university library, made it clear that the actual number of new members recruited by mid-November 1954 was 1,088 names which was a record number and overtook the previous year's total of 1,048 by the same date. Over 541 of these new members signed up to a life subscription, again a higher figure than the previous year. There was no doubt that this particular achievement provided the Union with a much more sustained attendance at its debates, particularly on the issues that were discussed. The Vice-President rightly stated that the membership drive must be attributed to the hard work done on the part of the college representatives to whom the Vice-President and officers and indeed the standing committee wished to record their thanks. The Vice-President's report went on to say that during the Michaelmas term the President's policy had been primarily to further the interests of good debating, guests not being invited merely because they were supposed to be a box office draw, and it was probably on account of this policy that the standard of floor speaking from the Union had undoubtedly been higher than in either the

Michaelmas term of 1952 or Michaelmas 1953. Most encouragingly there was an unusually good crop of maiden speakers who were selected to make their contributions to the Union during this term and it was hoped in the future too.

I can now conclude with an extract from my Presidential debate whose motion was entitled 'The English, like all good dogs, have had their day'. The extract is entitled 'Mr Wordsworth visits Stately Home and is much moved':

> Tax not the noble Lord with vain expense
> With ill-matched aims the architect who planned
> Albeit labouring for a happy band
> Of rain-soaked tourists only this immense
> And glorious work of rash extravagance
> Give all thou canst, the box is at the door
> Watch where you tread dry rot is in the floor
> Scarce thought the man whose zeal outstripped his sense
> And built these pillars spread that vaulting roof
> Scooped and bored into ten thousand cells
> In each of which a death watch beetle dwells
> Riddling the wood, crumbling the fabric down
> Behold the double meaning in the proof
> That a coronet is worth but half a crown.

Chapter 7

The Black Magician's Tale

JOHN WAITE AND I RETURNED in late January having had virtually three weeks touring the universities in eastern Canada. This was sponsored by the British Council and was clearly a goodwill visit as well as taking greetings from Cambridge to our fellow under-graduates in various Canadian cities.

We went as far west as London, Ontario which allowed us to go and visit Niagara Falls, hereinafter called Niffles as a point of respect and we were able, almost by accident, to visit Quebec itself at the invitation of the Governor General, the Rt Hon Vincent Massey. This enabled us to visit the Governor General's house Chateau Le Rideau and we also witnessed the activities going on in the Quebec parliament. The latter indicated substantial hostility between the French Quebec community and the Federal Government in Ottawa. Indeed, it was fairly easy to see that the activities of 1825-8 were not the last word in the matter of resolving the power of provincial parliaments.

It was also noticeable that the big University of McGill seldom had contact with the University in Quebec itself. We actually made this good in arranging a small tea party under British auspices to meet students from the French-speaking university in order to ensure that they were not ignored in our pattern of progress. We got much exposure on the media, I think partially because of the peculiar wit of Cambridge undergraduates and also because we had comical hats – nothing less than fine dark-brown curly brims provided by Herbert Johnson.

But the return to Cambridge brought with it the conclusion of my public activities at the Union, although John Waite was consequently to have his Presidency in the summer term, and we returned to college with the unkind prospect that we had nothing to look forward to but exams! That's not quite true. We had the possibility of trying to raise a boat for the May bumps although we decided not to do so for the Lent races which are rather too cold for comfort and in any case we had had a go in the previous year and secured the only bump in the boat club for that particular season.

The history tripos plodded along without too much excitement. Let's face it, the exams would be final exams and the amount of data covered was considerable and revising for exams is always a hit and miss prospect. I had one further problem which was that my standard of handwriting seemed to be below that acceptable to examiners and several times my director of studies brought me up short on the way in which I wrote. However, I was unable to lift the standard of writing to a satisfactory level in the time available. I shall return to this matter in due course.

Peter and I were much attracted to Harry Hinsley's lectures, particularly those on Hitler and Nazism, whereas I found mediaeval history even through the glowing lips of Ted Miller to be very difficult to grasp. However, we were very fortunate to have such assiduous dons in charge of us that I am sure we eventually did rather better than we might have expected. Nevertheless, when the exams came in early June I felt significantly more doubtful than Peter about holding my 2:2 which was preciously won in Part I of the history tripos the previous year. How right my forebodings were because when the results were published I had achieved a 2:2 but it was starred for illegibility. I thought at first that any exam that was starred in the Cambridge Tripos must be a matter of congratulation but when I found that illegibility meant almost certainly that my class was moved down, then it would appear that I had lost out on a 2:1 and ended up with a 2:2 which had very nearly been downgraded to a third.

At the same time as we were preparing for the exams we had also to take stock of the job market and try and get ourselves assessed for suitable employment. Cambridge University had a well-organised and thorough careers advisory system and we all went along at the appropriate time for assessment and invitation to meet representatives of the various industries concerned. Most of the large employers tended to be based in London, particularly where they were UK branches of international companies such as Shell, Esso, Procter and Gamble, and Philips. There was also the attraction of Civil Service careers to be assessed. With firmly entrenched northern roots I wasn't entirely happy about going into the great mass of London employees to chance my arm. I tended to think that a very large pool might prove an awkward one to swim in whereas a relatively small pool, for example major employers in the City of York, might provide a more secure haven. But this was perhaps underestimating the importance of these large international companies. As recruiters they took a proportion of graduates every year, whereas smaller companies based in Northern England might take relatively few graduates in relatively few years. But I was also engaged in a bit of a battle on what would be my ultimate destination in terms of ambition. The Presidency of the Cambridge Union had already started to open doors from broadcasters and journalists and I had met a number of people involved in these industries. On the other hand if politics was to be my ultimate ambition, and this was not yet finalised, then I would have to find some way of earning a living before I could expect to be taken as a serious contender representing those whose livings I was virtually unaware of.

Before I visited the appointments board I wrote a letter to Viscount Bracken who was Chairman of the Governors of Sedbergh School and asked him for the courtesy of advice on careers. I was invited to lunch in the offices of the *Financial Times* and another guest at the lunch was Mr C.M. Vignoles (Old Sedberghian) who was the Managing Director of Shellmex and BP. Brendan Bracken's advice to me was to 'go and see Mr Vignoles as he is sure to find some opportunity for you which will allow you to get your foot on the ladder.' Much as I was flattered by this advice I frankly didn't take it because I decided to find my employment in York which would strengthen the Yorkshireness of my appeal to Yorkshire constituencies which in the end I hoped to represent.

So it was that when Rowntree wrote to me asking if I could come along for interview with their graduate selection team on a due date, I readily accepted.

With hindsight this did seem to be a somewhat 'chickening out' operation. On the assumption that I had got a degree in history at Cambridge, together with the Presidency of the Union, the Secretary of the JCR etc., a rational person would say I should optimise this range of so-called qualifications and make sure that I made them work in the market place. It was also the case that by coming back to York to find a job with York's main employer, I was strengthening the links with my home. I obviously started to live there again rather than setting myself up in a flat in the middle of York and had free accommodation and meals provided in Huntington. But I suppose with two years previously in the Army, stationed largely in North Africa, to come back home was to some extent expected.

There was, however, another alternative which I also looked at quite carefully. The K shoe company of Kendal advertised and subsequently wrote to see if I would be interested in an interview in respect of a marketing post with them. The idea of coming to live in Kendal in the county town of Westmoreland as it was then, on the edge of the English Lake District, certainly had considerable attraction. I did go after it and for more than one interview, but ultimately it became clear that they really wanted someone to be trained up to deal with their retail shops in London and other main cities to market Gold Cross Shoes which they were importing from the United States. I had really no stomach for retailing, possibly slightly less for fashionable shoes, so we parted company although with some regret on my part. So I joined Rowntree in September 1955. By then I had equipped myself with a 2:2 degree in history, starred for illegibility. I had also been awarded the Joseph Larmor plate by a committee of dons and undergraduates at St John's as one who had made a singular contribution to the College during his time there. This large silver tankard is much treasured and will be passed on to my elder daughter, in due course, who was amongst the first women to be admitted to St John's College. She ended up as a double blue in cross-country running, where she took the course record, and in her coxing of the Cambridge boat in 1985.

I joined the marketing department at Rowntree in the autumn with several other graduates including Ken Dixon who joined from the Calico Printers Company a little later in the year. Rowntree was one of the great Quaker families who had founded an enterprising business in the late nineteenth century. Confectionery and cocoa were products that were not particularly well developed and had attractions for those of Quaker faith because of the highly nutritious value of chocolate and cocoa as a food and indeed as a drink, relatively modest price and an industry which had not been very strongly developed by the aristocratic families of manufacturing who looked elsewhere. The Quakers, however, took hold and introduced all kinds of policies designed to help their workforce keep fit, to provide medical and pension services and for many of them schools and villages to allow their lives to be of better quality than the average industrial life of the nineteenth century.

For many years the range of products was very similar between companies. Boxes of chocolates, bars of chocolate, various flavourings and fillings were marketed under the strong brand name of the maker such as Cadbury's Dairy Milk, Cadbury's Bourneville and Fry's Filled Cream Bar. Rowntree with its heavier overheads of social provision found itself in real difficulties in the late 1920s with a range of products which had a maker's name on it but nothing else to distinguish it from its competitors. Several hundred different units were provided on a long selling list but tonnages were modest, overheads were high and the need to provide products of a different type for the emerging markets in the 1930s pressed heavily on Rowntree. In 1929, so it is said, Rowntree was nearly broke. There then came a marketing revolution which is a textbook of marketing enterprise and excellence.

With the aid of market research (a novel assistance in those days), American advertising principles, broad imagery and with some ingenious product development Rowntree started to concentrate their efforts on producing original products. They did this with heavy advertising, memorable names registered for protection and a determination to enter various sectors of the confectionery market in a highly competitive way with all the goodness going into the product and no fancy frills or bows to provide presentational excitement. Famous brands on which the company has now built its fortune were

mostly marketed in this period between the wars. Kit-Kat, Black
Magic, Dairy Box, Aero and Smarties joined the original favourites of
Rowntree's Fruit Gums and Rowntree's Fruit Pastilles to provide a
formidable array of sugar and chocolate confectionery. The impact of
the brand names and the packaging was amazing when you consider
the Quaker foundation of the company itself. The Rowntree family
on the Board were asked for their support to agree to the use of a
name like Black Magic for their premier box of chocolates. The
twelve centres in the box itself were selected by a wide-ranging series
of consumer tests, not only to determine which of the sweets
consumers liked best but also which was the best version of that
individual flavour so that a chocolate could be designed to the highest
standards. The Rowntree Board was asked to agree to a product
called Black Magic which was set in a black box with small white
stripes. It was excessively smart and very chic and was designed by
the J Walter Thompson Company on the basis that women in
particular found 'the little black dress' an essential item in their
wardrobe in the 1930s.

Standards had been maintained throughout this period including
the original advertising which was frankly of a romantic kind with a
letter being written from a man to a girl which never quite finished
because the page had to be turned over. This romantic style of
advertising was also very alien to the Quaker tenets. A brand name
and advertising proposition were taken as essential ingredients of a
Rowntree brand and the advertising agent was as much a part of the
company's higher echelon as the company's lawyer. The marketing
team, therefore, of which I was a member, was engaged in
maintaining these standards and in developing them for the new
media of the day, e.g. television.

In 1955, as sugar rationing was relaxed, so commercial television
was born. The Rowntree company's very substantial holdings in
poster sites were changed and the money invested in television
advertising. I well remember the arrival of Mr Bernstein together
with his sales director Alex Anson by air at the airport at Rufforth
about 10 miles west of York. This was an exceptional visit and the
Rowntree Directors for marketing entirely supported the view that

we should shift virtually our whole advertising budget into the new and rapidly growing medium of independent television.

My interest in this side of the business grew substantially when I was made Assistant Advertising Manager in 1957. This involved me in visiting the advertising agencies in London who were responsible for the range of brands which were fundamental to the confectionery trade. They were the J Walter Thompson Company, S.T. Garland (shortly to become Garland Compton), and Ogilvy, Mather and Crowther, shortly to become Ogilvy and Mather. Garlands was the smallest agency who had dealings over many years on behalf of Peter Rowntree who was a Marketing Director for Rowntree's fruit gums and fruit pastilles. J Walter Thompson had the biggest brands – Kit-Kat, Black Magic, Polo Mints, Dairy Box and Aero. This was followed by After Eight Mints. This latter product was quite exceptional. It was launched originally as one of three packs under the After Eight name: a box of extremely fine chocolates at a high price, a pack of plain chocolate – two blocks banded together – and the peppermint creams known as After Eight.

After Eight Mints were a particularly difficult product to make. They involved finding a form of mint which when applied to the confectionery process would allow boiling to a high temperature to be followed by refrigeration, so that the centres became solid when they were coated with high-quality plain chocolate. After further refrigeration they were packed into individual brown envelopes, put into a carton and kept for some ten days in a cool environment to enable the cream to melt by means of an enzyme contained in the cream, so that they were liquid at the point of purchase. The placing into envelopes was done originally by hand with some assistance from a little jet of air to enable the envelope to be opened, so that the packer could slip the mints in and pack them into green cartons with the After Eight clock in gold. All three packs were presented as very expensive and very high-quality products and launched as a range. The launch took place in colour magazines and it featured various well-known members of society endorsing the product, including Mrs Cecil Boyd-Rochfort who was the wife of the Queen's trainer, Mrs Roy Boulting, the wife of the film director and others of that ilk.

Under the theme of 'luxury, unadorned luxury' they started to move up in tonnage in the market place. But soon it was shown that the After Eight Mint outstripped the others in this range to such an extent that this became the lead brand and the others survived for some little time, but in due course were removed to allow the peppermint cream to stand on its own feet with its very substantial sales record. The advertising, therefore, became entirely centred on the peppermint cream itself and the dinner table situation was the one that was primarily used under the theme of 'luxury, unashamed luxury'. Eventually the packing was mechanised and the envelopes were wrapped round the sweet, automatically cut to size and posted into the green box where they stood upright in slots provided by corrugated paper.

There was one other technical issue connected with this brand which was of particular interest. The peppermint leaf from which the peppermint cream was flavoured had to be of particularly strong flavour in order to survive the heat mixed with the refrigeration which was part of the process of preparing the After Eight Mint. The products research department scoured the United States and eventually found two farmers who grew Black Arm Mint on the slopes of Mount St Helens, the volcano, in the State of Washington. Both these farms were contracted to provide mint oil purely for Rowntree and this became a vital lifeline until sadly the volcano erupted and a cloud of ash settled on the ground in which the mint was grown. Nevertheless, a substitute provider was located in due course.

Whilst the marketing activity was considerable and the development of new and exciting products improved the market share, there were still important issues overhanging the confectionery and chocolate market. First was the fact that sugar rationing was still in place when I joined the firm in 1955 although it started to be relaxed during that year. The other issue was Resale Price Maintenance which was a long-standing agreement between the major suppliers that they would not allow their prices to be undercut by retailers, particularly big retailers or grocery companies, but had to sell at the price listed and only the price listed. This was challenged eventually as a restrictive practice, and after a considerable hearing in the Restrictive Practices Court under the judicial chairmanship of Judge Megaw it was held that Resale Price Maintenance was against the public interest and uncompetitive. This meant that if we expanded the sales force to include supermarkets and large companies it was more than likely that the prices of our products would be lower than those obtained in the confectionery shop, which had been the bedrock of the business for such a considerable period of time.

When I joined Rowntree the sales force called upon thousands of confectionery shops directly and other thousands of confectionery outlets were supplied by wholesalers. The distribution of confectionery was extremely high because it had been a rationed product during the War with total consumption which averaged 8 oz per head of population per week. This meant that the thousands of confectionery outlets were able to continue with a modest supply, but nevertheless a regular one, and distribution of products was maintained when many other types of products were not able to be obtained. This provided a bedrock of consumer consumption which was vital to the industry and allowed large volumes to be passed through to the consumer because of the high density of confectionery outlets known as CTNs or confectioners, tobacconists and newsagents. The industry was considerably discomfited by the decision of the Restrictive Practices Court but nevertheless there was no appeal. The inevitable happened, groceries and supermarkets became wide open for confectionery sales and although this resulted in a reduction of brand choice in many cases, the lower prices had a fairly persuasive effect on consumer uptake. Margins were tightened and it was becoming rather difficult to maintain the same scale of advertising backing the brands as had been available hitherto. Certainly for products like After Eight which had a higher price, reduction of price by supermarkets was to some extent at variance with the image of a luxury product. But in general terms the persuasive effect of the reduced price for a high-quality product was just as appetizing to the consumer as a reduced price on a normal product like a chocolate bar.

A career in Rowntree was not just confined to the four walls of the factory or administrative block. There were a lot of social activities which the company provided. There were playing fields galore and teams raised for a number of sports to allow competition in the York area. There was a theatre established and the Rowntree Players who were the main beneficiary of a particular investment by Joseph Rowntree. I found myself on the boards again in many plays and shows, not least of which was The Maytime Follies which each year produced a cabaret-style entertainment which was widely appreciated. A few miles from the company was the village of New Earswick, 50 per cent of whose population was permitted by the Company to live in subsidised housing. The village was managed by a Trust and it largely provided rented accommodation. It had a Folk Hall in which shows could be presented and this was the home of the New Earswick Gilbert and Sullivan Society. It was not long before they found they were short of a First Sea Lord for *HMS Pinafore* and as I was the shortest First Sea Lord they had ever seen, they kindly offered me the role. In the end I played most of

New Earswick Dramatic and Operatic Society, 1960. The author performing the role of Lord Chancellor in Iolanthe *with the chorus of fairies!*

those parts from Ruddigore to Iolanthe and thoroughly enjoyed myself.

In 1957 I took the first delicate steps towards a political career by standing in my native Huntington for the local council, the Flaxton Rural District Council. We not only stood, but the three of us who sought to oppose the sitting Councillors decided to espouse a Conservative label for the first time in local history. John Bowling, a farmer, John Bradley, a builder, and Giles Shaw, Assistant Advertising Manager at Rowntree mounted such an eloquent campaign that we were all three elected on the due date. This was the Council which my mother had been elected to in the 1930s and subsequently she was Chairman of it. Being by far the youngest of the Councillors I was gazetted to the water committee which I must confess was hardly the most exciting post but I understood their reasoning. After I attended the first meeting and was duly welcomed as my mother's son by the Chairman, he beckoned me to come up and we had a little chat. The water committee was all about land drainage and the establishment of sewage disposal services for the Flaxton District as well as the supply of water from the City of York Water Company. This white-haired gentleman, the Chairman of the Water Com-mittee, bent down from his high chair and said to me, 'Well Giles, there's a lot in drains tha knows, but bugger all votes' and I remembered that kindly exhortation which I suspect applied to many other municipal activities.

In 1958 I took a further step when some Old Sedberghians wrote to me from the town of Barnsley to ask if I would be interested in being their Conservative candidate at the next election. These were members of the Umbers family, whose family had owned and operated the Oakwell Brewery in Barnsley for many a long year. I went across to be interviewed by the Umbers family with Chairman Norman presiding in the Conservative Club which was, of course, supplied by Oakwell Brewery. They unanimously passed a resolution adopting me as candidate for the next election whenever it would come, but it was expected around 1959, so I duly drove off back to York.

On considering the matter overnight I suddenly realised that as I would have to take some time off for canvassing etc. I must inform my Chairman that the accolade of Barnsley had been placed upon my young shoulders. I asked for an appointment to see Mr Lloyd Owen, the Chairman of Rowntree. He was a very big man from the Welsh valleys with a lovely Welsh lilt in his speech and a large florid face which did not always remain in peaceful repose. I decided to come straight to the point and I said to the Chairman that I had been offered the candidacy in the name of the Conservative Party at Barnsley and I had indicated acceptance to the Barnsley Conservative Executive. Mr Lloyd Owen responded in loud tones. 'Barnsley, Barnsley,' he said, 'what do you think a Conservative can do in Barnsley? Young Shaw, you don't know how to earn your own living yet, how can you possibly represent others whose way of life you have no knowledge of? I tell you what, you work hard for the next few years and you can come back to me and talk about some other political opportunity when the time arises. In fact, Raymond Clifford is going to the United States in a week or two, you go with him and you can at least see how the other half of the world deals with chocolate. Now off you go.' So I tottered out.

He was as true as his word, so I wrote my resignation to Mr Umbers on Cunard notepaper (HMS *Queen Mary*) in September 1958. With hindsight the Chairman was quite right. Although I had certainly believed it necessary to build a potential political career with care, and over time, particularly when I was committed to fighting Yorkshire seats for at least my first attempt; Barnsley was not a bad name to conjure with. I also had my eye on the local seat of Thirsk and Malton in which I lived and I thus became involved in taking an active part in the Conservative Association. After the venture of gaining local authority seats I decided to become active in the Huntington Branch and eventually was elected to the divisional executive and in due course became elected Vice Chairman of the Association and thus one of the senior officers. This brought significant influence to bear on the Association and it also looked good on my CV should I offer myself as a candidate for selection in other constituencies in Yorkshire.

CHAPTER 8

The Common Marketeer's Tale

THERE WAS, HOWEVER, a major incident which affected the Thirsk and Malton constituency in 1957. At the Annual General Meeting, as is traditional, the long-serving Member of Parliament, Sir Robin Turton, addressed the members of the Association on a theme of his choice. It was well known that Sir Robin was a strong opponent to joining the Common Market. He therefore launched a vigorous attack, partially on behalf of British agriculture and partially, bearing in mind his Foreign Office service as a Minister of State, on behalf of the Commonwealth countries and the Empire overseas. He made it clear that he was against all progress to enter the Common Market and proposed that a motion to that effect should be drawn up by the Association to be sent off to the Party Conference, hopefully for debate. He then pulled out of his pocket a piece of paper on which he had drafted a motion which was strongly against any association with the Common Market, the major political issue at that time. As he read out his proposal a voice from the back of the hall shouted, 'On a point of order, Mr Chairman, he has come here in accordance with the summons to join the AGM but is it not out of order to propose a motion of this kind which is not on the agenda and which may seek to override the views of many other people who may wish to propose a different motion at the Party Conference this year?' There was a hurried consultation between the Chairman of the meeting, Colonel Harry Slingsby and John Rawson who was the agent for the Association. Mr Rawson's advice to the Chair was that certainly a special notice in advance must be given by those seeking to raise an issue not on the agenda for approval by the meeting. Sir Robin was considerably discomfited by this recommendation and considered it was unreasonable for the Member of Parliament to be sidetracked in this fashion. Mr Rawson, the agent, then said, 'In

response to Sir Robin, we could of course hold an Extraordinary
General Meeting to invite comments on the motion and alternative
recommendations for such a motion to be put to the Party
Conference, if members would wish.' There was a fairly reasonable
'Hear, hear' to that suggestion and although Sir Robin found it
acceptable he was somewhat disconcerted that his original motion
could not be put to the meeting as he had intended. It was agreed,
therefore, that an Extraordinary General Meeting be held at a date
convenient to Sir Robin in order to discuss the motions to be put to
the Party Conference.

After the business had been completed, the meeting adjourned and
there was a good buzz in the hall, reflecting interest in the soon-to-
be-held EGM. My good friend Michael Jopling and I felt we ought to
take advantage of this development to have a public meeting about
the European Community and a debate which might conclude with a
vote as to whether the members of the Conservative Association of
Thirsk and Malton would be in favour of joining the Community or
would be in favour of having nothing to do with it. It fell to Michael
and me to design some motions of a different character and to be
prepared to speak to the EGM and, if the Member of Parliament
agreed, to have a vote at the end of the meeting.

Accordingly, a meeting was held in Easingwold Town Hall and a
motion was put inviting colleagues to give their views as to whether a
motion which, like Sir Robin, opposed the Community so strongly
or a motion which supported our entry into the EEC was to be
preferred. We were astonished to see such a large number of people
in attendance; it must have been of the order of 300. Quite a bit of
lobbying was carried out prior to the meeting to ensure that people
who felt strongly, either for or against, should be well represented
and that there should be plenty of opportunity for them to air their
views. It was agreed that as a matter of propriety the Member of
Parliament should be allowed the first opportunity of putting his
views which he duly did with extreme force and a great deal of
personal commitment. Michael Jopling spoke next, in favour of
joining the Community and made the case for a motion which would
establish just that. I seconded this motion before the meeting and

widened the debate to make it plain that here was an issue on which we should all have a clear view at this time because it was going to affect our future. Indeed, it was the biggest issue coming before us for many years and there was no doubt that there would be a major debate on it at the Party Conference in the autumn. There were a number of speakers for each side of the argument and indeed the members in the hall got very worked up about the importance of the issue and many speakers wished to have their say. In the end, and with Sir Robin's agreement, a vote was taken. As far as I recall I believe that Sir Robin's motion achieved 120 votes and the alternative motion, in favour of joining the Common Market, raised 190 votes.

It was, therefore, declared that Sir Robin's motion was defeated and that the views of Thirsk and Malton Conservative Association should be noted as endorsing joining the European Economic Community. It was further agreed that a motion, properly drafted, should be submitted to Conference in the usual way. The motion in the name of Thirsk and Malton was chosen by the organising committee to be debated on the floor of the Conference. Michael and I were duly selected to propose and second the motion and there was much discussion within the constituency office as to how it might best be done without further embarrassment to our Member who had been in the House a considerable period of time and indeed was shortly to become the Father of the House. For Michael and myself this was a moment of rare excitement and at Brighton that year we basked in the national limelight of television and radio. It so happened that the mood of the Conference was reflected in the mood of Thirsk and Malton and the Conference motion was duly passed.

After the 1966 General Election, when Harold Wilson had obtained a more workable majority, Sir Robin Turton announced his decision to retire as the Member for the Thirsk and Malton constituency. A selection process was put in hand to choose a new candidate. This was a fairly long and tedious process but nevertheless I felt it right to put my name forward. This meant, of course, as Vice Chairman I could take no part in the selection process and as can be imagined a considerable number of candidates put in for the selection process in what was one of the safest Conservative seats in the North of England. Amongst the candidates offering themselves was one Jonathan Aitken who was seen as a glittering example of a Conservative dynasty, which had rendered enormous service to the Party both in peace and war. His father had been a Member of Parliament for Bury St Edmunds and his great uncle was the renowned Max Beaverbrook, owner of the *Express* group of newspapers. It was not surprising that Mr Aitken was regarded as a considerable catch and his profession at that juncture was that of journalist. He duly won the nomination and I came a fairly poor second to this illustrious Londoner.

Sadly, however, events took a fairly sharp turn when not long after he had been selected there were rumours running around that he had been involved in obtaining secret information from discussions with a constituent who was no less than General Henry Alexander who lived in Brandsby. He had recently retired from being involved in the Biafran War and it was on this issue that Jonathan Aitken wrote pieces for the *Daily Telegraph*, which indicated that he had obtained information which was not then in the public domain. Jonathan Aitken eventually found himself charged under the Official Secrets Act and arraigned in the Old Bailey for trial. This was not an enormous criminal offence but it was sufficient to cast doubt on the wisdom of selecting him to be the successor to Sir Robin Turton. The Association met to discuss what should be done, and there was general agreement that he should be invited to stand down forthwith from his post as candidate for Thirsk and Malton. The question of what was now to be done was quickly dealt with when Sir Robin swiftly announced that he had withdrawn his intention to retire and would serve the constituency for a further period of time. This was seen as an appropriate decision by the Member, although the runner-up to the selected candidate felt it might have been dealt with in another way.

Some years later when Sir Robin did indeed retire there was another selection procedure. Again, I put in my name on the not unreasonable grounds that I had come fairly close at the previous selection and as a local home-grown member of the constituency and not an imported member from down south or elsewhere I should still be judged by my peers. Amongst the applicants was a former Member of the House whose constituency had been abolished during the Boundary Review. It was in the City of Sheffield but he made a very plausible candidate as he knew so much about the House, both about being a constituency MP and what is more, representing a Yorkshire constituency. These factors were difficult for me to rebut in a manner which proved positive. Accordingly I was the runner-up for a second time and took note of the old proverb that a prophet is not without honour except in his own country.

I had joined the Bow Group and played a part in establishing a regional committee for the Group based in Yorkshire. Here I met a number of like-minded people who felt strongly about the European Community, including one John Bellak who was to become, together with his wife Prue, a very close family friend. He was also keen on politics and was hoping to fight a seat in Hull in the next election and invited me to help with his campaign if and when that time arose. It arose in 1964 and a number of us from Yorkshire, including my wife Dione and myself agreed to support him. He had been involved in the wool trade in Bradford and now wanted to make his first mark on the political ladder. We had some great times battering away at the doors in blocks of flats throughout the very long streets in Hull and it was clear that they had never seen a political candidate representing the Conservative cause. West Hull had once previously been held by a Conservative, namely Mr Richard Law, now the first Lord Coleraine who was the Patron of the constituency. He was the son of Bonar Law, the Prime Minister in the 1920s. I achieved a certain notoriety when the canvassing party got back to the constituency office at 335 North Road and it was discovered there were no keys available to open the door. Happily the downstairs loo had a half window open and I was designated small enough to climb through it. This was a substantial squeeze but nevertheless it was done and I opened the door from inside thus achieving much relief all round.

The West Hull brigade were a very happy lot and we soon became very friendly and although John Bellak did not win, he performed pretty well and the Conservative vote moved up a touch. I wasn't surprised when a year later, as the Conservatives in West Hull were awaiting the forecast Election date of 1966, they invited me to come to a selection process. This time I was successful and I became the candidate for the 1966 Election. My political teeth were well and truly sharpened in that campaign.

It started ignominiously when we had our launch meeting at a huge school built by the Socialist Council in Hull and when we filed in to sit at the table we saw there were only two people in the audience. I brandished my notes for my speech and said to the Chairman, 'Have I got to go through all this for all that?' At once he replied, 'Aye, you'll 'ave to go right through it because yon is the *Hull Daily Mail* and there'll be nowt in't papers if tha doesn't.'

So I duly eulogised the Common Market and committed myself to serving the burghers of Hull in the corridors of power. When I had finished some twenty minutes later the gentleman at the front from the *Hull Daily Mail* got up and left, leaving only one person in the auditorium. The Chairman of the meeting, Michael Gaster, was, I thought, a bit too generous when he suddenly said, 'Right now, any questions?' Up stood the remaining person and when he had uncoiled himself it was apparent that he was wearing rolled-down seafaring boots and was a very tall man. I somehow felt the image of the doorknocker of Number 10 Downing Street receding from my mind when he asked his first question. 'I'd like to ask the candidate's opinion of the Merchant Shipping Act of 1894.' 'I'm damn'd certain that's not in the candidates' guide,' I said to myself, but I stood up and said, 'I only know one thing about that Act and that is if it is as old as you say, it's high time it was repealed.' 'Quite right,' said the gentleman in the hall and I felt I had immediately doubled the Conservative vote. We had a chat with him after the meeting and he turned out to be the mate of a striking trawler in Hull docks and a lifelong member of the Labour Party.

Canvassing in the rain in Hull was a fairly miserable operation and several times we had to go down to the fish docks in the constituency to try and ply our trade with the trawlers. Wandering round the docks at 5 o'clock in the morning as the bobbers unloaded the crates of cod I felt considerably adrift. But when they started singing the Red Flag as I walked nimbly along the jetty I felt there was only one thing for it. I jumped onto a trawler, stood at the far end and conducted them in the rendering of that great anthem. This brought cheers from the trawlermen and I felt I may have touched the floating vote!

Despite this and many other incidents I succeeded in doubling the Labour majority single-handed but felt I had earned my corn and my somewhat damp accolade and I could now look to a seat which perhaps had a Conservative Member of Parliament and better prospects ahead.

CHAPTER 9

The Suitor's Tale

DESPITE THE SUCCESS of After Eight, the actual volume of the company and its position in the national market was not strongly affected. Indeed as the 1950s gave way to the 1960s the problems at Rowntrees like many other companies was to obtain a significant market share in order to be able to sustain high volumes of advertising in the face of new margin restraints brought about by the abolition of Resale Price Maintenance. For sometime Rowntree had been looking round for a partner and one of the more obvious was Mackintosh Ltd with whom they had established well-known overseas links for the manufacture of Mackintosh products under licence in the Irish company and indeed in Canada.

There was also a strong affinity between the two companies – both were Yorkshire based. The Rowntree family was Quaker in origin; the Mackintosh family was Methodist in origin. They both had strong Trusts controlling the businesses. They were both big-branded businesses. Quality Street for example was undoubtedly one of the greatest assortments ever offered and they had high public acceptance. But these things take a long time and other problems intervened (most notably an unwanted bid from General Foods in America) so that Rowntree and Mackintosh did not really get together until the late 1960s. In the early 1960s other important events occurred. It was towards the end of March 1960 that I had concluded a long week as Toad in *Toad of Toad Hall* with the Rowntree players. To recover from my week and my exertions I was most glad to receive an invitation from my Sedberghian friend, John Challoner, to spend the weekend with his family in Northumberland. I understood that his younger sister Juliet was likely to be there, a feisty girl of whom I was very fond. My brother Roger, bless him, who was always generous in these matters, loaned me a car for the weekend for the purpose of achieving greater effect! It was a Volkswagen Karmann Ghia, an extremely smart 'tart trap' somewhat let down by the fact that the engine was a normal VW Beetle engine of not much puissance. So off I went to Northumberland and had an excellent weekend to recover from my histrionics on stage and met a friend of Juliet's, namely Dione Ellison. She was shortly coming to London to seek employment in the interior design business and it wasn't long before I was making my way to the World's End where there was a small flat which she shared with another, clutching my box of Black Magic.

Being a cautious Yorkshireman, I took these things at a cautious pace. True, Dione did come up to visit my parents for a weekend and indeed we also managed a weekend at our house in the Lake District which was shortly to be sold. But it was not until July 1961 that I made the move to go and visit her parents in Ireland where her father was Professor of Astronomy at the Dublin Institute of Advanced Studies. He was a scientist and a very charming man. Whilst I was staying with them in their large Georgian house an invitation arrived for the Ellisons from the President of Ireland to attend a garden party at the Presidential Lodge in Phoenix Park where the President, none other than Mr Eamon De Valera, lived. It so happened that Professor Ellison was a close friend of De Valera because both were mathematicians and physicists. It was quite usual, therefore, that when there was a special occasion in Phoenix Park, Professor and Mrs Ellison would be invited.

During the weekend Mrs Ellison pointed out that Dione and I would not be able to attend the garden party at the Presidential House unless I was part of the Ellison family, making it clear to me that that meant we had to become engaged. Not that my intentions were anything but honourable, which they were, but I hadn't made any preparation for getting a ring. There ensued a hot rush to Dublin City to look for a ring. We found a fine aquamarine for the princely sum of £30 in Grafton Street, but again, being a canny Yorkshireman I hadn't got £30 on me! As an English cheque would be unlikely to be honoured, I panicked slightly about what to do. The answer was the Rowntree factory and the management thereof, namely Sandy

Miller who ran the company with both charm and success. I knew him well and so I rang him immediately. £30 came out of the petty cash and was rushed round to Mortons to duly acquire the ring. I then had to perform the duty of asking Professor Ellison for his daughter's hand. At first he was difficult to find, then he was quite difficult to converse with on this particular matter as his mind was on much higher things. I did eventually, however, corner him in his study and we had a modest exchange of views in which I said I hoped I would be able to look after his daughter and I quoted to him my present position as Advertising Manager at Rowntree together with my salary which I believe at that time was something princely like £1,900 per year. That matter was duly accomplished and Mrs Ellison was on the phone to the President's office to fix an extra couple of tickets for the garden party!

The occasion for this particular garden party was the State Visit of the Papal Legate from Rome. The Legate in question was an Armenian Cardinal named Aggaganian and the streets of Dublin were *en fête* because the visit of such an honourably high personage caused the Catholic majority great joy. There were banners across the streets and papal flags flying. I did notice one banner which I thought was particularly Irish – 'Long Live the Holy Ghost' it said. So I knew we were going to be in good company! At the Presidential Lodge we found the President, very tall and angular standing next to a very minute Cardinal resplendent in beretta and purple cloak receiving gifts. The Cardinal subsequently sat down on a gilded chair so that people could file past him and kiss his ring. I felt that I was no slouch in this matter and that on such an auspicious day I should go and get the personal blessing of the Cardinal and kiss the massive ring which was about four times greater in size than anything I had previously seen. Dione and I, therefore, duly filed up to gain his blessing. Frankly, I think I had done my whack and we retired home to Dunsink to consider our next move.

I felt that I should arrange a little celebratory dinner with the Ellison family. The Professor was not keen on going out to dine as he relied on Mrs Ellison to feed him in the proper manner when he wished. However, he was prepared to make an exception, provided

Long Live the Holy Ghost.

that we went to his favourite hotel, namely the Moira Hotel, which was to be found somewhere in the middle of Dublin but was not on the tourist list of exciting places to dine. However, it suited the Professor because he went in to dinner and waved away the menus and the maitre d' before announcing firmly, 'I would like a very extensive hors d'oeuvres followed by a large glass of brandy.' And so it was that the toast to our future life was proposed by the Professor in an extra large helping of Cognac and he would eat nothing more.

In due course we were married in London in March 1962 at St George's Church, Hanover Square, followed by a reception at 8 Hill Street, by courtesy of J Walter Thompson Company. We then spent a snowy honeymoon in Cornwall!

Our first home was to be a converted cottage in Easingwold, some 10 miles north of York. Dione restored the cottage and modernised it with the aid of Dickie Barugh, the builder, Walter Skillbeck, the joiner, and Ken Skinner, the plumber, a merry team. We had hoped that everything would be ready when we returned from our honeymoon but we had forgotten about the wintery conditions and in particular the gales from the North Sea. Walter Skillbeck, the joiner, came to explain why there were no doors fitted to the house. He said that the wind off the coast had prevented the ships carrying the wood from Scandinavia from getting into the port of Hull and, as he put it in his Yorkshire accent, 'If ever tha' wants to know when tha' was married, it wer' the year of the great wind.' But then Walter Skillbeck was a bit like that.

That was 'honeymoon' year. We built a lot of new friendships around Easingwold where our neighbours were particularly helpful and we were welcomed into its community. In 1963 the major excitement occurred with the birth of our first child, Henrietta Lucy. This caused particular pleasure within the Shaw family as apparently there had been no females born to the Shaws for almost 163 years.

The year 1962 was a difficult one elsewhere, especially at Rowntrees. In 1961 the Conservative Chancellor, Selwyn Lloyd, banged a duty on TV advertisements, and this effectively increased the cost of TV marketing by 10 per cent. Advertising budgets had to be looked at pretty carefully and some savings were made. More potent, however, was his decision subsequently to introduce a 10 per cent purchase tax and to increase that tax by a further 5 per cent in 1962. This was very difficult to absorb and resulted in a substantial fall in the total market for confectionery products. Nevertheless, the excellent brands which Rowntrees supplied and in particular the development of After Eight, gave the company very welcome relief from falling sales. Perhaps the advertising of After Eight as 'luxury, unashamed luxury' gave Selwyn Lloyd his opportunity to say that not all confectionery is an essential national food but some is clearly in the luxury market. Despite the purchase tax rise, After Eight was able to continue its development as a major brand at high volume and high profit.

In 1963 there was considerable activity on the political front. The era of Anthony Eden had come and gone after the Suez fiasco and then there followed the Prime Ministership of Harold Macmillan. He represented the last of his vintage within the Tory hierarchy and as one of those who came back from the War in 1919 he was something of a political force and brought high theatre with him whenever he spoke. However, in 1963 he fell ill and resigned. A fight broke out during the Conservative Party Conference in Blackpool as to who should be selected to succeed him. This caused real excitement when Quintin Hailsham renounced his peerage in order to stand and there was plenty of support for new candidates. However, such was the wheel of fortune that Mr Macmillan recommended to the Queen that she should send for the 14th Earl of Home as the best possible person to lead the Party and the Government at this stage. There was considerable fallout at this decision. Iain MacLeod for instance refused to serve under Alec Home and although the Earl of Home's reputation rested firmly on the Foreign Office where he had conducted himself extremely well after the Suez fiasco his knowledge of economics and his capacity to take correct decisions in difficult times were unknown. It was also unknown whether he could lead the Party through a tight election which was inevitably going to happen within a short period of time.

In the event Sir Alec fought a very gallant election but perhaps he had not been Prime Minister for quite long enough. On becoming

Prime Minister he renounced his peerage and was elected as Member of Parliament for Kinross and West Perthshire as Sir Alec Douglas Home. He was Prime Minister from 19 October 1963 until the General Election in October 1964 and having been defeated he then stood loyally by to help work out a new system for selecting leaders of the Conservative Party by an elective method. He finally resigned as Conservative Leader in July 1965, continued to serve in Ted Heath's government and was a much-respected figure throughout the land. So although Labour won they had a small enough majority to indicate that the wily Harold Wilson would probably wish to come back for another go at the electorate when circumstances appeared more suitable.

So West Hull was returned as a Labour seat with a larger majority. One of the consequences of all this was that John Bellak quite rapidly became the candidate at Keighley and the good people of West Hull invited me to take his place as the parliamentary candidate for West Hull in the likely event of a 1966 election. By this time our second daughter Victoria had arrived, so Dione was very much more involved looking after the children than in looking after the candidate. The arrival of Victoria also meant that our cottage in Easingwold was extremely crowded with little space for guests and friends. We therefore looked around for something not too far away but which would provide the family and ourselves with the grace and favour which we sought. Thus it was that we sold our cottage and bought a house in the village of Helperby which was late Georgian of about 1820 with lovely high ceilings including plaster decorations and which gave Dione the space to engage in real decoration and tasteful development. Once again we looked to local talent to provide us with our services. When we took Dickie Barugh, the builder, to have a look at the Helperby house it was still furnished with the predecessors' carpets and curtains. There was also an extremely large king-size bed with a mock velvet headboard in rich purple to match the bedside tables. He took one look around and said, 'It's 'ollywood come to 'elperby.' But as usual he set to work with a will. We found a very good local joiner, Mr Nolson, with whom I used to play dominoes regularly in one of the pubs, but as there were five in the

village I rather forget which one it was. I think it was the Half Moon.
Mr Nolson knew a decorator who turned out to be our next-door
neighbour and virtually single handed he did all the interior
decoration to a very high standard which satisfied Dione.

During 1965 my formal adoption as candidate for West Hull took
place. It was a pretty dour election, only enlivened by shafts of
sunlight from time to time when I saw a sylph-like figure in black
underwear through a glazed door in a row of promising Conservative
houses. I felt I should not approach but come back later for a more
interesting call. I came back later and knocked at the door. An old bag
opened it and asked what the hell I wanted. I said, 'Nothing, Madam,
but it would be very nice to know if you would care to vote
Conservative this time because I am the Conservative candidate.'
'Conservative?' she said 'In Hull? Certainly not!'

The result when it came was a resounding victory for the Labour
candidate, but for me it was a major lesson in campaigning and I was
very grateful for the effort which the local Conservative team had
made to withstand the Labour steamroller. That really concluded my
connections with Hull and although they were quite sorry to see me
go they were very glad to have a reasonable rest from elections.

So it was back to Rowntree with a vengeance and time to make up
for my absence on candidate duty. One of the big issues of the time
was the question of Resale Price Maintenance and whether or not the
major confectionery companies like Rowntree, Cadbury Frys and
Mackintosh would seek to defend the existing practices before the
Restrictive Practices Court. A deposition was made before the
Registrar in December 1965. The court proceedings, however, did
not begin until April 1967. The pressure to support the large supermarkets and others who cut prices to the consumers' advantage was
in Rowntrees' view offset by the reduction of the wide range of
choice, which would be threatened should price become the only
inducement to buy. The court found against the industry and Resale
Price Maintenance in respect of confectionery products etc. was held
to be anti-competitive and was dropped. One of the consequences of
this was that Rowntree looked about for genuine partnerships which
could strengthen the business and it was in these years, the late 1960s,

when active discussion with Mackintosh in respect of a possible
merger took place. Rowntree Mackintosh was formerly constituted in
May 1969. This also involved the expansion of business into Europe
and I served on the European Division Committee seeking to
establish new wholesale and manufacturing companies to broaden
and spearhead the sale of Rowntree Mackintosh products within the
Community.

So the 1970s dawned with a new company in place and with
international and particularly European objectives in view 1970 was
also an election year and a vital one because Edward Heath had
succeeded Sir Alec Douglas Home as leader of the Conservative
Party. His was a European cause and he was anxious to make amends
for the failure of the first British application which was largely due to
the obduracy of President de Gaulle of France.

Sadly, I had not found a seat in Yorkshire to satisfy my political
ambitions. However, as Vice Chairman in the Thirsk and Malton
division we had a major election on our hands with a new candidate
in the form of Mr John Spence. This all went very well and, despite
the absence through retirement of Sir Robin Turton, the Conservative cause triumphed and Mr John Spence was duly elected with a
large majority. Sir Robin was Father of the House and on his
retirement was ennobled as Lord Tranmire.

It was some eighteen months later that the opportunity I had been
seeking turned up – the member for the Pudsey division, Mr Joseph
Hiley, announced that he would not be defending the seat at the next
election. A candidate selection procedure was, therefore, held and I
duly presented myself to the selection committee. This was chaired
by a large, corpulent gentleman, called Mr Philip Simms JP. When I
had settled myself down in my seat, he stood up, stared at me fairly
quizzically and then said, 'Right, Mr Shaw, now why Pudsey?' To
which I said, 'Right, Mr Simms, why not?' There was a titter round
the table and the President remarked, 'I told you that was a daft
question, Philip, and now you've got a daft answer.' However, the
questioning was resumed and on the whole it was quite amicable.

There were, however, a number of keen candidates on this list and
it was with considerable relief that I got to the final selection of two

with Keith Hampson. He had previously been selected as the
candidate for the Ripon seat on the death of its long-serving member
Sir Malcolm Stoddart-Scott. As by-elections are very tricky matters,
and the Conservatives were not in the ascendant, Hampson lost
Ripon and had put in for the Pudsey seat which was next door. The
final selection for Pudsey was to be held in the Civic Hall under the
television cameras of Yorkshire TV. Pudsey Civic Hall was built with
the proceeds of a court case when the Borough of Pudsey sued the
City of Bradford for refusing to provide compensation for their
withdrawal from Pudsey of the right to levy a water rate. Two elegant
QCs fought the matter out. Pudsey was adjudged to have been a
victim as far as the City of Bradford was concerned and they were
required to pay appropriate compensation for the removal of this rate.
That enabled Pudsey to have a sum such as a quarter of a million
pounds which they promptly decided to utilise on the building of a
Civic Hall, rather than let it fall prey to Leeds on the loss of Pudsey's
Borough status.

It was in this fine new building that Hampson and I duly performed in front of an audience of well over 300 people and
eventually the votes were taken and I was pronounced the winner.
On subsequent enquiry it would appear that the majority I won was
pretty slender. Nevertheless, I had won and became the candidate for
Pudsey in the Hall and in front of many thousands in the TV
audience.

So now the die had been cast and I think I was right to go and see
the Chairman of Rowntree, who had succeeded Mr Lloyd Owen,
namely Mr Donald Barron, to advise him of the fact that it was likely
I would fight the next election in a seat which I could probably win.
He was very generous in understanding my position but wanted to
make it clear that he would have preferred me to stay with the
company. Nevertheless, he understood that this was a long-held
ambition, that the sentiments were right and that a seat like Pudsey
would probably find me a very useful and committed individual to
keep the flag flying for the Conservative Party in that somewhat
surprising part of West Yorkshire.

I set to work to get to know Pudsey, this amazing place and its even more amazing people and spent a lot of my time in 1973 doing just that. In many ways Pudsey was an unlikely Tory seat. It was an old mill town with many still in operation and having a substantial industrial workforce based on the old Yorkshire textile industry. It was a Borough seat and the Borough itself was granted to the town by a Charter signed by Queen Victoria a few months before she died. In fact, locals always believed that the effort was so great that she died because she signed the charter for the Borough of Pudsey.

In 1972 during Ted Heath's government a new Local Government Bill was introduced creating metropolitan cities and metropolitan county councils in the areas of West Yorkshire and in many other populated areas in the country to increase the size of local authorities and to provide them with a broader range of services concentrated in the one authority. In order to make way for these changes the Tories abolished many of the Boroughs in West Yorkshire and their powers and services were transferred to the Metropolitan City above them. This provoked a severe backlash when I became an active candidate in 1973. If local government means anything at all, it means that those with responsibility for local government should be local people, and that the organisation should be controlled by a council elected locally so that they all felt they had a strong influence in how the Borough performed. Moreover, the Boroughs of West Yorkshire were intensely proud of their status. It fatally undermined their confidence to remove the Boroughs at a stroke and take local powers away to the Metropolitan City, which was so disliked by the Pudsey folk, who were independent and not prepared to love Leeds or Bradford simply because they were quite close.

CHAPTER 10

The Pudsey Tale

IN 1972 THE BOROUGH OF PUDSEY was not unlike many others in West Yorkshire which were associated with the wool textile business. There was the River Aire running through the middle of the Borough and also the Leeds-Liverpool Canal. On one side of the River Aire was the Borough of Pudsey itself and on the other were the two Urban Districts of Horsforth and Aireborough, the latter being composed of three townships, Rawdon, Yeadon and Guiseley. This was a substantial geographical divide and to some extent it proved quite difficult to get people to cross from one side of the valley to another for subjects such as constituency events or meetings. This also indicated the degree of commitment which inhabitants had to each of the sections of the Borough in which they lived. There was a loyalty there which, if tapped, could be of great value in building a constituency in the future. The situation of Pudsey was interesting too because it came between the two large cities of Leeds and Bradford; indeed it might be mentioned that if there was anything between the two great cities of Leeds and Bradford then Pudsey was it.

At first sight it did not look particularly helpful Conservative territory. The economy had been traditionally based on the wool textile industry and by 1974 there were major problems with maintaining the health and profitability of textile companies against the advance of man-made fibre. But Pudsey had some traditional mills which were able to keep going despite the pressures of changes in fashion and some decline in the heavy woollen industry with the widespread growth of domestic central heating and lightweight clothing. Bradford mills had also welcomed immigrant labour from Pakistan and other overseas sources who readily took to weaving and became an essential part of the new textile economy. Looking around my new-found constituency I was not overwhelmed by the prospects of a high Conservative vote which somehow did not look well aligned with a landscape of many mills. Nevertheless, in the end I was pleasantly surprised by the number of Conservative votes that came out of the areas where industrial workers lived.

In 1973 I was engaged in a whole series of activities and meetings to get to know the people on either side of the valley and to try and avoid suggesting that one area was better than another and one series of potential Tories was better than another. It was a matter of flat-out campaigning when the whistle blew. And with the candidate selection taking place in December 1972 we reckoned that it was likely the General Election would come within eighteen months. In the event it came earlier, in February 1974. The election had been over-shadowed by a lot of difficulties for the Conservatives. There were strikes, there were three-day weeks, there was even an injunction to clean one's teeth in the bath and consequently there appeared to be some difficulty for the Government in trying to contain events. As it happened the Government had a fairly workable majority of seventeen but the country was very ill at ease with being mismanaged in this way. Finally when the Police were unable to control the striking miners and public disorder near the Birmingham gas works at Stetchley, Mr Heath decided to go to the country on 'Who runs the country?' and seek a further endorsement. In my view this was a hazardous undertaking. The Government had an adequate majority, they just needed to govern better.

But there were two major issues which affected Pudsey in particular on both sides of the valley. The first was the decision under Peter Walker's Local Government Act to dissolve the City Boroughs and to amalgamate the local government of the area into the big cities of Leeds or Bradford. This was a body blow to the pride of Pudsey and was felt just as keenly in Horsforth or Aireborough where the local sitting councils were dissolved and both the Urban Districts were absorbed into Leeds. This was something extremely difficult for me to defend, particularly as the newcomer I was not well attuned to the importance of having local councils staffed by local people who could readily respond to public pressures on the things that really mattered: snow clearing, pavement repairs and easy access to departments such as planning and housing, which was so fundamental to the quality of life. The other big issue was the possible threat of a motorway extension from the M1 across between Leeds and Bradford through Pudsey to join the A1 at Dishforth. This became known as the Pudsey-Dishforth Motorway and was the subject of violent opposition from all my constituents on either side of the valley.

My predecessor, Joseph Hiley, was selected under rather different circumstances. The first candidate that had been selected for the 1959 election was the Hon Rowland Winn, the eldest son of Lord St Oswald. He was an extremely active and experienced journalist who had spent his twenty-first birthday in a Spanish jail during the Civil War of the 1930s. He was under sentence of death, but being a spectacular linguist and a great conversationalist he was able gradually, to talk his way out of this extremely difficult position. He had not been long selected as the candidate for Pudsey when the inevitable happened and his father died. Thus Rowland was translated into the Lords as Lord St. Oswald before he could be a political candidate in the House of Commons.

The second choice was a local lawyer of some notoriety. He apparently had won a court case and had a considerable celebration in a local hostelry and then was arrested by police going the wrong way round a roundabout in his car. Bearing in mind they had not much time, the Pudsey Executive tried to find a local solution, and they found a very good one. The Lord Mayor of Leeds, 1957-8, was none other than Joseph Hiley who was a resident in Horsforth in the Pudsey constituency and for many many years a local businessman in the textile industry with companies operating in Yeadon within the constituency. The two most senior Tories from the Executive went to visit him one Sunday afternoon to see if he could be persuaded to take up the challenge. Joe's wife, Mary, noted the arrival of Henry Thompson the President, and Bill Crabtree the Chairman and said, 'Joe, you'd better go to the door, there's Henry Thompson and Bill Crabtree out there.' 'Aye,' said Joe. So he went to the door, opened it and said, 'Aye. I thow't you'd coom, you'd better coom in.' So they all went in to the dining room, sat round the table and discussed the possibility that after his retirement from his mayoral duties he might allow himself to become the Conservative candidate for Pudsey; he had already fought an election in Leeds West in 1955, so he was an experienced candidate. Joe was always a thoroughly loyal man when it came to the Party and the Party clearly needed him and the local party in particular. So with an appropriate amount of reluctance he agreed to their proposal, provided that the campaign would not start until he had finally finished his mayoral year in May 1958.

He was the faithful member for Pudsey from 1959 until I took over the candidacy in 1972. Being a textile man he was well known within the industry. He was never a great one for meetings or things like that. The correspondence he had with people was probably not as great as his personal visitations, frequently on Sundays after church, as Joe rather expressly reminded me. He had lived locally most of his life although he was born in West Leeds and went to school there. He had certain rather charming habits, one of which was to change his shoes at 4 o'clock every day from the locker provided in the House of Commons because that marked the 'end of the shift'. From my perspective it seemed it would be very difficult indeed to try to become as good a local member at Joe Hiley. I wasn't a local Leeds person and I couldn't pretend to be; nor was it likely that I would be as comfortable living right in the middle of the constituency as Joe Hiley was, who actually started living there during his industrial career; nor would I wish to try and maintain a reputation as well established as that of Joe, being the local man born and bred. But I could possibly start my career in politics on a slightly different level, either on the national scene or perhaps even in Government. So we set out in January 1973 to canvas as much of the constituency as we could, getting to know the Conservative Clubs, going round the factories and that kind of thing. Preparation well in advance can be an important contribution to any campaign.

The history of Pudsey itself has been well documented by local historians and the book has been published and during 1973 I became acquainted with Pudsey folk and their past traditions. The intensity of this relationship, between and MP and the folk and traditions of one's constituency is, I feel, a much undervalued thread in the larger tapestry of the political and social life of this Kingdom. It is fair to say that its reputation in the nineteenth century and early twentieth was not of the smoothest place. Indeed, it was credited with being a home of witchcraft and certain activities were undertaken which indicated a certain hostility to people coming to visit Pudsey or to seek to move there. Moreover, the borough of Pudsey was split up into a lot of small enclaves which were regarded as special units in their own right. Portions of Pudsey town are divided between Upper Moor and Low Town and Green Top and Chapel Town and Farsley, a town in its own right, and Swinnow where a great deal of municipal building had taken place, in Thornbury and Fulneck. The latter was one of the most enchanting places within Pudsey and was a small village which was largely built by the Moravian sect when they established their presence in Pudsey in the seventeenth and eighteenth centuries. There is a beautiful Georgian terrace overlooking the Tong valley and along it was built not just a village but two schools, one for boys and one for girls, and never the twain should meet, because the chapel was in the midst of the two schools and kept them apart!

The reputation for rough behaviour within the various sectors of Pudsey Borough involved the practice of a number of old traditions. Despite the massive presence of St Lawrence's church it was, for many years, not a church licensed to solemnise weddings for that right belonged to the ancient church in Calverley, dedicated to St Wilfred. This gave rise to a common tradition that the lucky groom on his way back on his horse to Pudsey would be subjected to missiles being thrown at him to see if he could be knocked off his horse on his wedding day. There were also many incidences of people seeking to move into the area who were diverted from so doing by the roughness of the inhabitants towards 'incumdens'. The use of the ducking stool for awkward women was also established. In the nineteenth century, Pudsey was well known outside the Borough for the fact that birds had to fly backwards due to the appalling soot given off from the smelting of iron and for there being treacle mines in Pudsey. The smelting and the soot were certainly fact, one being the consequence of the other. But looking from Fulneck in the

Presenting the keys of the new minibus to the Horsforth Ladies Lunch Club.
Left to right: Councillor Margaret Frame; Councillor Maurice Crosfield; Mrs
Roland Barrett; the author; Mrs Val Stephens.

nineteenth century there was a lot of shale mining and some smelting and, of course, the arrival of textile factories with factory chimneys. There is little doubt that there was a lot of pollution which is very evident but whether the birds ever flew backwards to get out of the way of it must be regarded as unlikely. The treacle mine has no positive identification but it was a well-observed belief that

The first hilarious moments occurred during the debates on amendments to the Prices Bill which the Secretary of State introduced. The first one, if I recall correctly was to do with food subsidies and related to the first clause of the Bill. The first amendment read 'Clause 1, Line 1 after butter insert "cheese"'.

Paul Channon was leading for us at that time, the amendment was duly moved by the Secretary of State, and Paul Channon rose and asked a question. 'Would the Right Honourable Lady kindly tell the Committee what kind of cheese.' This put Shirley Williams into a slight fluster because on the whole she rather expected everybody to know what cheese meant and from that point of view she felt it was rather a devious question. So she answered it by saying, 'I am sure the Right Honourable Gentleman is very much aware as to what constitutes cheese in this country, it is a milk fat product which has been prepared and consumed for many many years; it has a high percentage of butter fat and the English have a fine range of cheeses which I think would be suitable for subsidy in times like this.'

Paul Channon asked a second question: 'I fully understand the Right Honourable Lady's close perspective of what constitutes cheese and I am sorry if my question did rather upset her but I might perhaps re-phrase it. Could I please ask the Right Honourable Lady whether she means that the French producers of Camembert, for example, would be suitable for subsidy, the Italian producers of Gorgonzola, Dolcelatte and possibly the Dutch providers of Gouda – are we to provide from the English Exchequer monies to actually offset some of the costs which these alien providers of alien cheeses currently send us with monotonous regularity?'

The Rt Hon Lady duly stood up to address the Committee and conceded, 'There may be a problem here on which I would like to take further advice, so I will willingly withdraw the amendment and return to the Committee with an appropriate answer to the Right Honourable Gentleman to whom I am most grateful for taking such a considerate view of some of the problems associated with subsidy assistance.'

Having expected this particular amendment to be over in a matter of half an hour it took two and a half days before the actual matter was resolved, when the Rt Hon Lady, the Secretary of State for Prices and Consumer Affairs came back to the Committee with a new amendment which said 'after butter insert cheese of the hard-pressed Cheddar type'.

I thought that we did a jolly good job for consumers in this country as well as for the Exchequer by preventing that particular sloppy presentation of the list of foods covered by the subsidy regulations. The tedious element in the Bill was the long process which it took to go through the House of Commons. This was particularly due to the Opposition who decided we might try and run this Bill to annoy the members of the Labour Party by having to sit overnight to consider it. Our problem was that we wanted to have a Bill where we could demonstrate our parliamentary force, but the Prices Bill was really not much cop for the boys at the back, whereas those of us who were involved in the Committee had a fairly reasonable understanding of the Bill when we eventually got it back onto the floor of the House. In the end we managed to get enough chums to come and speak on this particular matter about which they knew nothing to keep the House up right through the night. In fact, it has to be said that it went through the morning afterwards and did not actually cease until something like 3.30 the next afternoon. I believe this was a record for that particular Parliament and possibly stood the time for several other Parliaments as well. It merely shows what can happen when half a dozen keen and competent members of the Opposition are determined to try and carry a parliamentary measure through a long period of time to upset the Government, and in particular the Secretary of State who found herself having to have a large number of Labour Members kept up all night just in case one of us was to try and get a vote taken on one of the amendments. This is political witchcraft at its worst, or at its best depending whether you are in government or opposition.

It was not until 1978 that the Labour Government began to crumble. Strikes and three-day weeks and erosion of the Labour majority all made it possible for the Conservative opposition eventually to topple Jim Callaghan's government by one vote. That was indeed a highlight if ever there was one. In fact that was not a

Conservative vote but it was a Northern Irish Republican from Tyrone who determined to come in person to abstain despite the efforts by the Labour Whips to keep him happily occupied in the main bars of the House until by voting time he decided somewhat quixotically that abstinence was his real calling!

A second phase was government when Mrs Thatcher achieved office in 1979. For eight years I was a Minister in five different departments, starting in Northern Ireland which was a fascinating experience although my activity was mainly concerned with the economy which was, of course, in a very difficult state. As well as getting to know the Reverend Ian Paisley and other local leaders I became fairly heavily involved with Mr John Z. De Lorean and a certain famous motor car. Whether that was a high point or a low point, history will no doubt judge but my duty was to ensure that the plant was built on time and that the production of this brushed-steel tart trap arrived in its American market in sufficient quantity. Needless to say it didn't and I was transferred to the Department of the Environment.

Here my main responsibilities were in planning, but also the water industry and I must have been quite good at this because I was transferred to the Department of Energy to become the Minister for Coal, just as we were planning to deal with the next miners' strike. This was undoubtedly my most exciting period as a Minister as I frequently had to answer questions raised in the House, particularly by Tony Wedgwood Benn or Dennis Skinner. We kept the coal flowing and as the strike started as late as May there was never any serious shortage of power. It was, however, a desperate and bitter dispute with the mineworkers and caused the collapse of the union as well as a considerable amount of disorder. I was then moved as Minister of State to the Home Office with responsibilities for the police. I remember spending my birthday in riot gear marching through a village in South Yorkshire where barricades were on fire and missiles were being hurled. A consequence of this was that I had to carry through a new Public Order Bill in order to bring up to date the provisions of the 1936 Act. This was a major task with the Labour Opposition on the Committee led by Gerald Kaufman MP. Finally, as

'Mr Yorkie' by Roger Gale.
Reproduced by kind permission of the 'House Magazine'.

Minister for Industry I was involved in the privatisation process for the nationalised undertakings, a very sad affair, particularly within the shipbuilding industry. But we were able to start the process of rebuilding British Leyland into Rover Group which has now turned into such a substantial success.

My third and final phase between 1987 and 1997 involved the Chairmanship of Standing Committees on Bills and an active role in the 1922 Executive of the Parliamentary Party; also the Chairmanship of the Select Committee on Science and Technology which somewhat surprisingly got me involved in the excitements of human genetics. The Committee visited several countries abroad, but mainly the United States, where we saw a number of companies and universities at the forefront of biotechnology. Select Committee work is one of the most fruitful areas for backbench Members of Parliament, and I am sure will develop strongly in the future. I was also appointed by the Prime Minister to be one of the members of the Parliamentary Oversight Committee on the Security and Intelligence Services – fascinating.

A career in parliament can be both exciting and interesting: one thinks of the outbreak of the Falklands War and indeed the Gulf War. It can be extremely tedious as the hours spin away far into the night with votes on the Maastricht Bill and it can be riveting as we heard Geoffrey Howe's resignation speech and its effect on Margaret Thatcher. Margaret's own speech on the day that she announced her resignation was a tour de force which will certainly stand the test of history. But MPs are wise if they recall that whatever they do and whatever they think, their power purely rests on the votes of their constituents. Pudsey today is a very different place. Whilst its original economic base has declined it has gained hugely by the expansion from Leeds as a whole, as far as employment and prospects are concerned. The constituency has a large commuter population, a great diversity of excellent schools and a population that has been steadily growing. Through force of history and individual personality its communities have maintained their independent characters and their separate identities. Although there are major problems in the pressure of traffic and road planning together with the pressure on

Former Prime Minister Sir Edward Heath as guest speaker at the annual dinner of the Pudsey Constituency Conservative Association, 1975. Left to right: Henry Thompson, President; The Rt Hon Edward Heath MP; the author; Philip Simms JP, Chairman.

green belt for new house building and other developments, I believe the future looks much more promising than it did when I first became the MP in 1972.

After Mr Wilson had won the election of February 1974 he was operating on a very thin majority and it was fairly obvious that he would seek for an opportunity to increase it by returning to the country, let's say in the autumn. That was the case and he obtained a larger and more comfortable majority.

CHAPTER 12

The Minister's Tale

I WAS HONOURED to be invited to join the Conservative Government in 1979 and to serve through the first two Thatcher Administrations. Margaret, as is her wont, certainly kept me on my toes. I started in Northern Ireland, and when, after 18 months, the prisoners went on hunger strike, I was *moved*. I then went to the Department of the Environment, where I spent two years with responsibility, for among other things, the water industry. We had the first national water strike ever, and I was *moved*. Undaunted, Margaret tried again and off I went to the Department of Energy, with responsibility for the coal industry. The miners then struck, and I was duly *moved*.

Following that, with even greater courage, Margaret moved me further up the picket line, to the Home Office, with responsibilities for the Police. I had not been there too long before we had riots on the streets, and I was *moved*. But such was Margaret's magnanimity that she sent me to the Department of Industry, which I have to confess, was not noted at that time for ministerial longevity.

When at my request, I returned to the backbenches after the 1987 election, it was with a memory bank of unique and happy experiences in five different Departments of State, under seven Secretaries of State, for which I was profoundly grateful.

Northern Ireland
It was Michael Jopling the Chief Whip who rang shortly after the successful election in 1979 to invite me on the Prime Minister's behalf to join her Government. He said, 'Giles, that's the good news though it may not be so good when I tell you that she wants you to go to Northern Ireland.'

I responded to him that I thought there would be little doubt that

111

The Family, 1978.

with Dione's long Irish connections through both her parents, her
father being born in County Wexford and her mother being born in
Armagh city, we would be happily disposed towards taking out the
Northern Irish portfolio from its dust cover.

I was summoned down to the Northern Ireland office in London
forthwith to meet Humphrey Atkins, the Secretary of State and my

fellow Ministers on the Northern Irish team. Humphrey had been the Chief Whip in Opposition and he issued our instructions. I was to be allocated the two departments of commerce (which was industry, trade, inward investment and EEC matters) and agriculture (which of course included fishery matters as well as land drainage). Whilst this was not an unusual appointment for a new Minister it was somewhat unusual that two of the largest departments should be selected for being bracketed together under one pair of hands. I was also given a great long briefing paper on each department and was introduced to my Private Secretary, Jennifer Taylor. I completed the appropriate forms in respect of the Official Secrets Act and indeed swore to it and finally I was issued with a car and a most reliable driver named Susan. We were due to meet up and catch a plane from Northolt the following morning.

Within the first few days of being posted to Northern Ireland I went to call, as was correct, on the Permanent Secretary of the Northern Ireland Department, Sir Brian Cubbon who was a very experienced senior Civil Servant. He was particularly knowledgeable about the Irish issues and was the victim of a terrorist attack when he was accompanying the British Ambassador in Dublin. Their car was blown up by the IRA. The Ambassador, Sir Ewart Biggs was killed and Sir Brian was badly injured. Now better and returned to office, he gave me an excellent briefing on the Irish scene and indeed the terrorist issue first.

We discussed the NIO (Northern Ireland Office) which was the Government Department spawned by Westminster to oversee the administration of Northern Ireland having dissolved its powers to run itself. The headquarters was in Whitehall and the NIO administered its Department largely through the work of the Northern Ireland Minister and the Northern Irish Civil Service. He pointed out that the reign for Northern Ireland Ministers was over and moreover with the shutdown of Stormont went the structures and powers for local administration too. The Whitehall-based Ministers, therefore, were responsible for the running of the local councils and the individual departments, as well as sharing in all the security duties which Ministers had to undertake. He emphasised that Ministers were the first, and in elected terms, the only line of real authority in the Province. In his view a junior minister in the Northern Ireland Department had wider powers than a junior minister in any of the other Departments of Government. We might be labelled junior ministers by the London-based national press, said Sir Brian, but in Northern Ireland a Minister was a Minister and a Minister was part of Mrs Thatcher's government. The Irish population was used to having Ministers of its own but to have all its own departments run by a team of Westminster-based Ministers gave it an access to Government which the population never previously had. It went without saying that the administration was required to administer to all the citizens of Northern Ireland whether they were catholic or Protestant. It also had a special relationship with the Government in the Republic through the Foreign Office, and there were special relationships with the EEC in respect of less-favoured areas which included all the Province of Northern Ireland.

I soon discovered that Jennifer Taylor was quite exceptional and she had worked in the Department of Agriculture herself for many years having previously been appointed PS to Labour Ministers; it was also one of the most complex. She warned me that the scale of activity in both these departments was substantial but that the Agriculture Department was extremely well staffed and led by a major figure in the Northern Irish Civil Service, Jimmy Young, the Permanent Secretary. He certainly was very well established and probably the most experienced of all Permanent Secretaries in the Northern Ireland Department.

We had to make good contacts with him and his senior people and establish a system which would provide me with the briefing necessary to have a fairly close working idea of how the department operated and who were the key figures within it. My problem was compounded by the fact that I had absolutely no knowledge of agriculture as a government department or indeed an industry. The Department did, of course, have offices spread throughout the Province and a programme was soon arranged to enable me to go to each of the outstations in turn. Inevitably there were close contacts with the EEC department in Brussels. European regulations and problems in connection with farm subsidies, agricultural laws, fisheries and so on were to become a regular diet of the papers in my red box. Actually it wasn't a red box because red boxes were thought to be a security risk as they indicated that I was a Minister. Frequently I was to be found travelling on scheduled air flights to and from Belfast and instead of a red box I had a black briefcase like so many other Northern Irish civil servants.

The Department of Commerce on the other hand was another department with a very wide remit, being responsible for inward investment, so crucial to employment as well as energy which was a vexed issue with the current issue of possibly closing the Belfast town gas works. The problem here was that no alternative arrangement had yet been made and the Department of Commerce had ruled out trying to obtain some kind of piped gas supply from the UK national grid which already spanned Scotland, England and Wales.

It is typical of Departments and indeed of changes in government when skeletons come out of the predecessors' cupboard. In this particular case there was much time lost in failing to seek alternative arrangements which meant we had nothing to offer in return for the closure of the gas works which all parties agreed was far beyond its sell-by date. I had no alternative therefore but to authorise the decision to close the town gas supply, with a substantial period of time before it became effective, in which searches for alternative systems, including the possibility of mining lignite in the Province itself should be looked at again in order to try and find an effective alternative.

Inevitably I had to give a press conference on the closure and because I had no replacement plan to offer I had produced a feeble excuse of the kind which holds no water whatever – namely to say that you can't have every single aspect of UK life replicated in every part of the United Kingdom. This was leapt on by the Rt Hon Enoch Powell who issued a statement that the Minister for Commerce had now made it clear beyond doubt that he regarded the citizens of Northern Ireland as second-class citizens, who must not expect that every aspect of UK energy policy could apply throughout the Province as it did through the rest of the United Kingdom. This was, of course, a somewhat overstated position because what we might hope to do was to find an alternative supply in due course when we could afford to handle the costs of installing such a line across the Irish Sea. It was well known that the Government of the Irish Republic was extremely keen to develop such a scheme and could have some resources to put towards it.

Nevertheless, the *Belfast Telegraph* led with headlines: 'Minister accused of stating that people who live in Ulster will be second-class citizens and must not expect to receive energy supplies in the manner that the rest of the UK will be able to receive them.' However, I reacted very angrily at what had been said because I understood its political weight and damage, coming as it did from Ulster's senior politician at Westminster. Sure enough Mr Powell raised the matter during Prime Minister's Questions, once again making it clear that one of her Ministers had made a decision which inevitably made the citizens of Northern Ireland second-class citizens in the matter of energy supply.

For me, however, it made the present position and any future position very difficult if this point was to be left unrebutted. I demanded to see the Press Officer from the NI office and stated that I wished to make an apology about this particular position as soon as possible, with television coverage as well as press coverage. This was greeted with a flat refusal and the comments that Ministers do not apologise, particularly when they are making policy decisions which cannot be refuted. I persisted with my case and then took it to the Secretary of State, who agreed that I could try and have it done, adding that it should be as soon as possible to be effective.

Happily I was addressing an audience of the Chamber of Commerce when it was arranged that television coverage would be given and I duly made my apology. I suppose I had invented for myself the policy of grovel to try and reduce the damage and luckily it succeeded. No one was more pleased than the Rt Hon Enoch Powell who used his new-found authority on these matters to rise at Prime Minister's Questions for the second time in the week to congratulate the Prime Minister on this firm decision and handsome apology which had now been offered to the people of Ulster by one of her Northern Irish team of Ministers.

Although I wasn't present on that occasion those who were said that Mrs Thatcher looked both startled and pretty angry at having a Minister grovelling around on television apologising for announcing a policy decision which she fully supported. This little episode had its political downside, yet I do not regret having gone through with it in this way and I suspect I took a rather more mature view of the importance of establishing a certain credibility as a Minister in Northern Ireland, rather than to just go through the motions of rubber-stamping every decision just because the previous government had endorsed it. In this particular case no plans had been made, so it was not possible to disclose anything other than the bleak closure of the plant itself. Technically there could be no solution to this problem unless it was an 'all-Ireland' initiative when the two governments might quite genuinely have come together to make provision for energy supplies in a mutually satisfactory manner.

Meanwhile the De Lorean car project absorbed a considerable amount of my time. The negotiations had been completed by the Labour Government and it was our task to get the factory built and operating as soon as possible. On the face of it the De Lorean motor car which was designed exclusively for the West Coast of the United States had a lot going for it. The very attractive design was of Italian origin; it was powered by the Renault engine which was so successful in Formula One; the transmission system was designed by Colin Chapman of Lotus; and a former director of production at Aston Martin was in charge of the development. We succeeded in getting the land adjacent to the Dunmurry Golf Course which was a greenfield site; this allowed a factory to be designed and developed with a view to having labour attracted from both the protestant and catholic communities. Indeed there were special entrances designed for just that purpose.

The question of costs however rapidly raised its head. A board was formed to oversee the De Lorean company's investment in Northern Ireland and the Department of Commerce had a nominee upon it, but it was a complicated arrangement. There were several companies in the De Lorean group, one in particular having been raised in the United States with the purpose of inviting distributors to sign up to take the De Lorean car, provided that they invested in the company itself. This appeared to be successful, for something like two years production sold well in advance by this method. But despite the engineering skills of Colin Chapman, anxiety began to arise in respect of the total quality of the production and testing of vehicles.

In a nutshell we did not allow sufficient time for the final checking and testing of the quality of the vehicle before we were committed to ship the first orders to the United States. In part the reason for this was to get some cash flowing back from the market to try and assist the horrendous level of debt which was being piled up. From my point of view, the task we had been set was to deal with the erection of the factory and form the commencement of the production, and we had been able to achieve this in a relatively short period of time. Perhaps we had not given quite enough thought to the fact that this would be a Northern Irish workforce handling a type of project on which they had rarely, if ever, had to work before. Although the Northern Irish had had plenty of experience in engineering, shipbuilding or indeed of aircraft manufacture, this kind of high-quality car had to be produced with an absolutely unblemished appearance to attract a high sale in the showroom at a high price. Some batches had to be returned, while others raised doubts but I think a nod and a wink let them through. In consequence, therefore, the buyer in many instances found the car unreliable and not as highly finished as the marketing presentation would warrant. In addition to this there were doubts being raised about De Lorean himself as a man of integrity as well as a man of vision. The vision thing seemed to me to be alright – the question 'Is he able to form and drive a team to reach the quality standards demanded?' was harder to answer.

It was decided that we should try and float the De Lorean company in the US Stock Exchange at the earliest possible date. This again was to broaden the catchment area so that shareholders would come in and relieve the foster mother, the Government, of underwriting the project. This was a hazardous undertaking because of course the car had not as yet achieved a reputation in the market that was blameless. Nevertheless, it was thought by Goldman Sachs that a project of such novelty would attract a certain type of investor who might not put his money into General Motors but would like to see a hefty return on a high-risk but dazzling project. The fact that approximately two years' worth of production had been pre-sold gave us some encouragement of this view. I went over to the United States for discussions with Goldman Sachs and I think at the same time I met a number of potential investors.

One of our main advisors in the United States was the British Consul General in New York, Sir Gordon Booth. His knowledge of the American market was unrivalled and his contribution to handling investment projects from the US into Northern Ireland was extremely impressive. He agreed that the project had a reasonably high degree of risk attached to it but pointed out that De Lorean had been involved in taking high-risk decisions in General Motors and had created for himself a very good reputation for getting a number of them right. When he quit General Motors to go private he published his book *On a Clear Day you can see General Motors* as a fairly scathing testimony of that company. We probably underestimated the complexity of the De Lorean motor organisation and its various companies and the arrangements which had been made with Colin Chapman which appeared to end in numbered accounts in Swiss banks. But nemesis was round the corner in a somewhat unlikely form.

A backbench colleague at the House of Commons having long been a strong critic of the De Lorean project was particularly critical of the amount of money that had been poured into it and was deeply sceptical that it could be returned in the shape of a two-seater gull-wing motorcar. He had been in New York and had met a secretary who worked in the De Lorean office who suggested to him that this man was up to all kinds of tricks and should be thoroughly checked, so he wrote to Margaret Thatcher quoting this source of evidence. The Prime Minister was away in Australia and her office, somewhat unwisely, sent the letter off to the Attorney General as it seemed to indicate possible illegality. This hit the papers, including those in New York, under the headline 'De Lorean Company Referred to Attorney General', which was enough for Goldman Sachs to recommend pulling off the plans for an early flotation. This was, of course, quite unknown when I met De Lorean and his wife Christina Ferarre for a splendid dinner at the Jockey Club (or the 21 Club). He was the smoothest host imaginable and when accompanied by this vision of a woman it was a night to remember.

About this time Ulster was ravaged by the effects of the collapse of the textile industry and in particular the man-made fibre industry. The attractions of setting up a plant in Northern Ireland were pretty major: excellent workforces, development grants at a high level, strong industrial ethic, and its location within the UK. Many big companies were already there and were well established: ICI at Killroot; Courtaulds at Carrickfergus; Du Pont near Londonderry and several other firms like British Enkalon. The collapse in this industry was dramatic and devastating.

The need, therefore, to increase efforts to find new developments which would come and locate in Northern Ireland was very much increased. The only one which was brought to our attention was the Lear Fan project, the product of an extremely successful aircraft designer named Bill Lear. He had died at the height of his fame with the Lear Jet, one of the most successful executive aircraft in the United States. His widow, however, had the project and the designs that he worked out and I made a trip to Reno, of all places, to see her and find out whether she might be interested in locating this project in Northern Ireland. The main features of the aircraft were that it had two engines which drove a very large four-blade fan at the rear of the aircraft at considerable speed, made of a light, strong carbon-fibre product known as epoxy graphite. This was very tough, very light, and was produced by a spinning process not dissimilar to that involved in artificial fibre work. I thought this might be a possible alternative source of manufacture for those who were being forced into unemployment by the collapse of the fibre businesses.

At the time of our interest in the Lear Fan project the Federal Aviation Authority had not yet pronounced on whether they would license it, but after a lot of toing and froing and some considerable delay, despite having had some success in convincing MOD and HMG that this might be an investment worth looking at, the FAA turned it down on the belief that with two engines and a single gearbox, there could be real difficulty if the gearbox went down. In point of fact, in Lear's opinion the lightness of the aircraft allowed it to fly at 50,000 plus feet, and because the fuselage and wings would be made with very strong resin material it could be flown at considerable speeds so that if the engine cut out its glide path would be enormous. Frankly I didn't like the sound of that too much. But the refusal of the FAA to license the aircraft meant that there was clearly no future in it for us although Shorts were interested in the carbon-fibre process for aircraft parts.

Meanwhile I picked up an inward investment for the Agriculture Department. This was a company called Schreiber who made cheese slices to go with the universal McDonald hamburger to provide the cheeseburger. Northern Ireland had a very rich supply of milk which contained a high level of casein which was appropriate to this type of cheese. I went all the way out to the Schreiber Company which was located on the shores of Lake Michigan at Green Bay, Wisconsin. It seemed to be perpetually dark there and I remember being woken up at 5.00 a.m. to go clumping round the cheese factory. This was a brisk business, well run and with a chief customer as large as McDonalds there was no reason why they should not be interested in developing a project in a good agricultural district close to the market of the United Kingdom. This one eventually got through the system satisfactorily and I believe it is working well in Northern Ireland.

The Agriculture Department, which included fisheries, did have grave difficulties during this period. Fisheries in particular were in decline and this was largely due to the declining stocks in the Mourne fishery stretch between the Northern Irish coast and the Isle of Man. European fisheries regulations were applied and it was considered that the fishery should be closed until the stocks had built up properly again. I was therefore tasked with announcing this very sad measure, which prompted a delegation from Mr Enoch Powell whose constituency, Down South, included several of the fishing ports. He brought a delegation of fishermen from Kilkeel to the Department of Agriculture, so I went down to meet this distinguished former Minister who introduced me to these big men who wished to air their grievances. It was one of the things about Enoch that he was an extremely courteous man, dressed as ever in his black suit and Homburg hat; he always referred to me as 'Minister' and a long and amicable discussion ensued about the tragedy that was now befalling his fisherfolk. We had a full and frank exchange of views and he fully understood the huge importance of allowing the stock to recover if there was to be any hope of continuing the fishing industry in that part of Northern Ireland.

Soon afterwards we had a row with a very well-known importer of foodstuffs, Marks and Spencer. The Permanent Secretary of the Agriculture Department, Jimmy Young, came to see me concerning a product which Marks and Spencer made and had recently been imported. His point was that the cheese with which it was coated was made from unpasteurised milk and was thus against food regulations for Northern Ireland. I asked him what he felt we should do and he thought a hefty letter from me might do as the first shot of what might be quite a considerable exchange of views bearing in mind the size of Marks and Spencer in the food industry. A letter was duly sent and an invitation for the appropriate director to come and visit us in Northern Ireland was duly offered.

The reply indicated that whilst he was very pleased to meet me he did not think a trip to Belfast was necessary but rather an invitation to visit M&S at their headquarters in Baker Street and perhaps to view their research outfit which was brought into play on matters like this. So off we went to Baker Street and quickly resolved the problems of the Cheese Cannelloni. That particular stock of product was withdrawn from Northern Ireland and replaced by a different recipe which would meet the Department of Agriculture and Food regulations. We then went to the research establishment where they were trying to measure the ideal sugar content for yams. This, no doubt, was for their Brixton branch but it indicated how far M&S would go to find the ideal product to meet the tastes and appetites of their British customers. Henceforward they did the same for Northern Ireland customers too.

In addition to looking after the departments every Minister in Northern Ireland was expected to carry out duties on behalf of the team, indeed there was a Minister on duty every night and a Minister on duty every weekend. In the latter case it was possible to invite one's wife and children to come out for certain weekends and to live in the maisonette which had been built for Roy Mason at Hillsborough Castle. This we duly did on several occasions including one which I remember with some poignancy – the morning Earl Mountbatten was killed whilst boating in Southern Ireland. This tragedy burst on the duty Minister and I was he. There was nothing frankly we could do but I rang up the Secretary of State and asked him if he wanted me to do anything out of the ordinary. His suggestion was that we might offer a surgical team from Belfast's Royal Victoria Hospital which was particularly well skilled in dealing with explosions and burns to be sent down if the Irish would wish to have it. We did make the offer but sadly it was too late. In the afternoon we arranged a picnic on the Mountains of Mourne and together with our police escort we set out on what we hoped would be a slightly better afternoon than the morning. Halfway through the picnic we heard the undoubted sound of a big explosion. Through our police escort we soon got to know what had happened – a landmine had been detonated at Warren Point and fourteen British soldiers were dead. It was a hell of a day.

By contrast there were some lovely days when we went to agricultural shows or spent a weekend again with my heavy mob in full attire, ringing shearwaters on one of the Copeland Islands off the north coast.

The time passed rapidly as I constantly rushed by plane from the mainland to Aldergrove and back again, sometimes in the day, and it wasn't long before, as we were discussing the problems of the chemical industry in Northern Ireland, the call came from Downing Street – I was to be off to the Department of the Environment in the morning to take on a new posting.

Department of the Environment
Compared with Northern Ireland and all its activities the Department of the Environment was a fairly dull choice, one of course which wasn't mine. My responsibilities included Land Use Planning

and the Planning Inspectorate, minerals planning, the water authorities – soon to become companies – the London Docks Development Corporation under the Chairmanship of Mr Nigel Broakes, pollution and waste disposal. I was also to take on the traditional role of Denis Howell, namely Minister responsible for flood hazards and any other climatic disasters. I was perhaps slightly misled in my view – there could be some big issues flowing from these assignments.

First was a national water strike, which had never happened before, so it was a unique matter and it caused very considerable disturbance to the Prime Minister; it was national and it was over pay. Tom King and I had to parade at Number 10 at 8.00 a.m. each morning with the latest figures for those who were having to use stand pipes in the absence of the public supply, and answer the question of how supplies were being made up, how long the strike would last and what negotiations were taking place. Strike management then became a clear part of my responsibilities and it was not easy in an industry which was as essential as this and yet wasn't organised as well as some others when it came to union negotiations. There were after all a lot of private water companies and local authorities had a strong role in the sewerage system and obviously were concerned about the introduction of stand pipes to provide water to their populations. Although South Wales was strongly affected not all the members of the unions concerned came out – frankly the negotiations were soon concluded and the strike was gradually withdrawn. Nevertheless, it was an interesting incident.

The London Dockland Development Corporation for the re-building of much of Docklands was a very interesting responsibility. Michael Heseltine had been strongly influenced by how Baltimore had recovered part of its docks into a fine environment for new buildings, domestic housing and offices etc. DOE officials went over to take a thorough look and to find out whether such a formula could be applied to the London Docks whose wartime ravages had never been properly restored. This resulted in the Isle of Dogs being the source of an entirely new scheme, not just of restoration but of replanning large portions of that city area. This had to have the open support of the local authorities which was not always easy to obtain

Mrs T's Bookmark.

although that fine Labour colleague who sat on the Docks Board, Bob Mellish, was a tower of strength in trying to get Tower Hamlets to speak to Deptford, Newham and Southwark, and vice versa. The scheme basically was to construct an attractive area for commercial activity as well as housing so that new businesses could be drawn to the docks to provide new jobs in an area of very high unemployment and to reduce the congestion in many areas of the City of London.

One of the first industries to take advantage of this area were the newspapers of Fleet Street who saw the opportunity of building new plants which might be able to be operated with far fewer workmen than was the case at that time. Indeed, Fleet Street was always under pressure from strikes, from chapels, and from union leaders who wanted to use their power to disrupt and threaten publication overnight of the morning newspapers. (This eventually erupted as a major strike causing large-scale public disorder in a very congested part of London. But that was a matter for the Home Office, of which more later.)

We duly had floods in the spring and I was sent to York, my own home town, to clump around in a pair of leaky Wellington boots trying to look diligent in making the waters go down. I had good relations with the water companies and we enjoyed developing them by sending teams of accountants round to establish profit targets within fixed limits of expenditure. A lot of opportunities for efficiencies were discovered and on the whole the privatisation of the water companies was a great success. I was involved in the appointments of Chairmen and other posts in most of these companies which had been transferred from local authority ownership to shareholder ownership. It wasn't too long, however before a regulator had to be appointed to ensure that all companies were providing sound value and sound investment to repair their ageing plants.

I had a modest joust with Mrs Thatcher who had been advised that the DOE was about to introduce legislation which would take away the well-known right of local authorities to assume responsibility in their area of sewerage treatment. Actually this was a recommendation of the Monopolies and Mergers Enquiry. Armed with the report and with a marker on the vital page I went to Downing Street full of hope

if not of glory. Her researcher who was present, I think was called
Ferdinand Mount which didn't fill me with excitement. I explained
to the Prime Minister that the Monopolies Commission recommended that the right of local authorities to claim responsibility for
sewerage treatment etc. was in their view a non-competitive practice
and they recommended that the right be rescinded and that local
authorities should be invited to tender in the usual way. 'Let me see
it,' said the Prime Minister. She said that in a fairly firm tone and as I
moved forward to give her the volume it slipped from my hands onto
the floor. The small marker of the page in question fell out and I was
left with the unpleasant duty of trying to find the page in a volume of
some 2,000 pages! This resulted in my great confusion. 'Give it to me
and I'll find it,' said the Prime Minister. 'Perhaps I could give it to Mr
Mount as he might enjoy reading the report.' But I assured her that it
was there and that the recommendation should be implemented.

Department of Energy

I was appointed Minister for Coal, with responsibility also for
Nuclear Power, under Peter Walker. He told me to get to know Ian
MacGregor quickly and try and understand what his reactions would
be as the crisis surrounding the coal strike approached. The Department, as was its practice, was getting ready for its annual miners'
strike which previously the union had won hands down. This was to
be a more carefully planned operation – stocks were already high and
they were being pumped higher as month succeeded month.

It was likely that the issue upon which the miners would strike was
not pay and conditions as was usual but Mr McGregor's long-term
plan for the industry entitled imaginatively 'The Plan for Coal'. This
was the long-awaited assessment as to profitability of pits and the
need to close those which could not be made profitable. The industry
was well aware of these long-term preparations and there had already
been some discussions about the profitability of existing pits in all the
main mining areas; a concentration of investment for example had
been made in those pits which showed profitable returns and not in
others. But the scale of the problem in the coal industry was such that
when the total plan was laid out it caused very real concern to the

mining industry. I found the members of the Coal Board and their staff extremely interesting and they had some fine graduates assisting them in the developments for the next phase. But mining is a long-lived industry and changes of this magnitude are pretty awkward to sell. Nevertheless, Peter Walker's first step in this direction was to revise and to get the Government and Treasury in particular to approve a new National Mineworkers' Redundancy Scheme. Its benefits were increased substantially to allow £1,000 per head, per year of service over the age of sixteen. As mineworking regularly threw up thirty or thirty-five years of service for miners this scheme clearly was a major influence on the way in which miners looked at the possible threat of redundancy from 'The Plan for Coal'.

Another main influence was to ensure that there was no disruption on the railways to enable coal movements to take place during the strike. Traditionally the miners had looked to the NUR to help them in these circumstances but this time it looked pretty unlikely, although there was a sudden anxiety about wage claims which had the Railways Board on the verge of a strike. Happily the matter was settled.

The strike, when it came, did create enormous problems concerning pickets and the containment of picket violence on private land at the entries to collieries. There were flying pickets coming up the motorways from one area to another and the police were sorely stretched to contain the scale of the dispute. Reinforcements were brought in to the mining areas from other police forces and in many cases the Metropolitan Police supplied additional numbers. This did not go down too well in South Yorkshire or West Yorkshire where the Metropolitan Police quickly obtained a reputation for rough handling of people and strong-arm tactics, but as predicted, the month of May was not the best time for the miners themselves, either to rally support from other industries or to threaten in any real sense the power supplies which were so reliant on coal.

We met with the Prime Minister each morning at around 7.30 a.m. to let her have the full details of the scale of supplies at the power stations and the amount that was moved during the course of the night or the previous day. This was a very significant figure but it

Minister of Energy visits Caphouse/Denby Grange colliery, Barnsley, September 1983.

Mr McGregor and Minister.

relied upon a handful of railway signalmen to let through the supplies at places like Coalville in Leicestershire and other special junctions like Shirebrook in Nottinghamshire to ensure that the coal supply from the UDM mines was getting through successfully.

Keeping an eye on Ian McGregor was almost more difficult. This was particularly so when he was needed for television interviews with Arthur Scargill which he sometimes refused. For some reason he took a shiner against his personnel chief, Ned Smith, who virtually walked out on him and took the train back to Canterbury where he lived. We wanted Ned badly for an interview with Scargill because he knew more about the coal industry than Scargill did. He couldn't be traced on the railways, indeed we couldn't find him until he got back to his home, far away from the studio. We were unable to bring him back so McGregor was forced into a debate that he really wasn't well suited for and walked out halfway through. This was the sort of thing that caused a rumpus from Number 10 and, of course, made McGregor look particularly silly. Almost as silly as when he started wearing Sainsbury's shopping bags over his head to disguise the fact he was the man he was. But we did have some long discussions together and I much admired his deep Celtic soul and his devotion to Scotland.

He actually had a house where the Crinan Canal joins the Straits of Jura and he went up there as often as he could to sit in the twilight watching the seals come up and contemplating on the issues of the day. He told me once that in his times in the mining industry in America a strike had occurred at a mine in Wyoming which frankly was never settled and, as far as he knew, it was still going on some eight years later. But he was much more sanguine about the outcome of events in the UK industry – the Redundancy Scheme, the fact that the stocks were so high and that May led to June, the fact that there was no support from other allied unions, such as the railways, the fact that the UDM had broken away from the NUM and was now a bastion in the most profitable coal fields with a long life ahead of it, all took their toll on Scargill and his men. The issue of policing and containment of the picketing was very galling to the miners who had never had this kind of coverage of policing before. This undoubtedly had its effect on the morale of the miners.

In the end of course the NUM lost this particular battle and the industry lost its battle to maintain its strong militancy against its owners. But I had quite enough of marching through mining villages with burning barricades and the effect on the local mining communities was dreadful. It is that legacy which was probably more important than the political victory which the Government had won.

As I had responsibility for the nuclear industry as well as coal, I made a number of visits to Sellafield and other sites run by BNFL. Sellafield was a source of very considerable irritation to those who wanted to undermine the nuclear industry. The Irish were always complaining about the discharges from its outfall pipe, and the local population had a natural anxiety about it because a leukaemia cluster had clearly been identified in the area of West Cumberland where the company's site was established. I decided to make a visit and to arrange for a bit of publicity, hopefully in favour of the company and its works. I elected to go for a swim not far from the outfall pipe in order to demonstrate that it was perfectly safe; local television were signed up to come and record this magnificent gesture. It was to take place early in the morning so that it could be on the Breakfast Show of Border Television. When I got out from my hotel in Seascale I discovered that the tide was miles out, but nothing daunted I ran most of the way to where the tide was starting to come in. The camera crew however were utterly exhausted and whether they got any decent pictures of me flopping about in the water I frankly do not know.

During the period of the miners' strike regular reports had to be given to the House of Commons and of course many Opposition Members put down questions for Private Notice and answers had to be given to them. In the case of Peter Walker's absence on duty or on holiday I had to answer for him. This was more difficult than it sounds because the niceties of the coal strike meant that a lot of constituencies were adversely affected and the extent to which local communities were damaged was very difficult to answer whilst the strike was still going on. The Department did have a very good team to try and obtain up-to-date information of where the real problem areas were located and I was well supplied on rising to answer questions. But standing at the box it is always very difficult to know how to answer long questions and when it is best to use a short answer or an even shorter one. I had an occasion when Mr Dennis Skinner rose and asked a very convoluted question indeed which lasted three or four minutes. It was not possible to answer it as one question but I merely said to him 'No, sir' and sat down. He paused a little time and then he sat down too. I heard the Prime Minister lean over and say, 'Well done, Giles,' and I began to think that Section 137D of the Local Government Act had been forgotten.

The Home Office

And so it was that I was appointed Minister of State to the Home Office in 1984 and joined Leon Brittan, the Home Secretary. My responsibilities were for the police and for broadcasting and it also included civil defence. At first sight it was merely moving me up the picket line, so to speak, because having the whole of the national police force to deal with gave me a great opportunity of meeting different officers and Chief Constables up and down the country in the shortest possible time.

With the unravelling of the miners' strike police forces in many cases were bloodied, but unbowed. I cannot think of a single police force whether in a coal mining area or not which hadn't been involved at some point in the actions to be taken to try and contain this strike. Reinforcements were always wanted and had to be summoned from police forces elsewhere. The response was very variable in terms of the number needed, but the speed at which the respondents had to come was of primary importance.

In addition to the miners' strike there had been a number of major incidents involving the police reacting to public disorder. The most substantial was that in Brixton which occurred over two days in April 1981. The Home Secretary appointed Lord Justice Scarman to make an inquiry and to report on it, which he did by November. It was a thorough-going inquiry and it had significant recommendations to put before the Home Secretary, who by then was Willie Whitelaw.

There was much claim that the police had acted with excess, particularly against racial minority, and Brixton was not the only scene of public unrest. In July there were serious disorders in Southall, in Liverpool (Toxteth), in the Mosside area of Manchester and in the West Midlands. All had major impacts on their communities and the role of the police in each was one of trying to restore public order which in many cases had turned into looting and arson. My main task therefore was to establish close relations with each and every force I visited and to some extent express appreciation for the outstanding way in which they had dealt with events which were unexpectedly thrust upon them. But in many cases the police had lost the confidence and support of their communities for the robust way in which they had handled events during the miners' strike. This was particularly true in Yorkshire, South and West, where communities felt very bruised by the police activity. The building up of community and police relations therefore was an essential objective and it would take a considerable time.

Lord Scarman also made a number of representations about the existing Public Order Acts (passed in 1936) and the way in which they may have outlived their usefulness. Problems of stopping people and searching, particularly when mobile in a car, the problem of what is actually a riot and how far it can be distinguished from an affray or from public disorder suggested that a major new piece of legislation might be required. This came when Douglas Hurd assumed responsibilities as Home Secretary in 1985 and a new Public Order Act was commissioned. It was my task to take this through the House of Commons with the minimum amount of delay, hopefully in cooperation with the opposition parties. This I was able to achieve by having full discussions with my opposite number Gerald Kaufman and providing where possible, agreement on some of the key issues which he was concerned about, in return for allowing a relatively speedy passage without the Committee sitting through the night! Whilst parts of the new Bill were strongly attacked there was no doubt that the cooperation which Gerald Kaufman offered was an essential ingredient in its ultimate success.

There was another issue in which I was involved which was one of real tragedy. There was a major fire in the Bradford City football ground at Valley Parade. The back gates of the ground were found locked in order to prevent other people entering when the ground was already full and this resulted in significant loss of life. I was up in Yorkshire that weekend and having had a word with the Secretary of State I met the Chief of West Yorkshire Police at the ground at 5.00 p.m. that evening. Some of the stands were completely burned out and the scene was absolutely ghastly with bodies reduced to charcoal. I reported the scale of the disaster (fifty-six dead) to the Secretary of State, Leon Brittan, and he took an instant and extremely important decision. He said he would appoint a judge to carry out a thorough inquiry into both the *causes* and the *consequences* of this disaster, and he had in mind then to bring forward legislation which would ensure the safety of sports grounds as part of the Government's contribution to making public safety a feature of the design and administration of those who ran sports grounds. By Monday morning he had appointed Sir Oliver Popplewell, a Judge of the Queen's Bench Division to head the inquiry and to make recommendations as to how safety could be improved and what legislative steps should be taken. Thus within a matter of a day or two, the people of West Yorkshire knew that there would be a major inquiry into this disaster and a promise of legislation to ensure that such tragic situations should not occur again. This was a rapid decision taken by a very capable Secretary of State.

The consequences of the Popplewell Inquiry were many and the whole question of the seating at sports grounds, the way crowds were handled on the way in and on the way out, rules to provide that gates should at all times be kept open, or at least openable on touch, the question of the numbers to be admitted to various sections of the ground and also the drive for all-seating sports grounds were key recommendations. I was very glad to be associated with this work despite being deeply saddened at the tragic loss of life which initiated it.

Reverting to the policing, I was extremely keen to develop crime prevention as a major contribution by the public to the police force to ensure that they did their bit to deter those who commit crime. We established a Crime Prevention Council, and we had important meetings during the course of the year to ensure that all the police forces were able to contribute in a way which the public would respond to. The concept of Neighbourhood Watches was an important element in this formula and I am very glad to say that there was a rapid response from most areas to participate in that particular development. I think police forces were genuinely keen to find an opportunity to work more closely with their local communities in a field which both the public and the police saw was valid and well worthwhile.

On the broadcasting front I managed to stimulate the development of community radio, or local radio as it is now called. The availability of parts of the spectrum for use on local radio for short distance transmission allowed companies to apply for licences to broadcast and to start up a large number of companies who made profitable use of the opportunity to broadcast. Most of these stations were dependent on income from the sale of advertising space but the BBC also set up a range of local broadcasting companies which were a very successful development of their public service principle at the local level. There was opportunity too for cable development but this was rather slow and did not have the degree of commitment from the private sector which we thought worthwhile. Nevertheless, a range of cable companies was set up and the long slog of beginning to lay cable network started in these years.

I had one amusing incident when Mr Robert Maxwell came to call because he wished to buy a cable company. The only company he was interested in was one in the Windsor and Maidenhead area which he judged would include London airport. He could obviously see a benefit here in establishing conference facilities for international business to come and call and use the broadcast media as a quick way of establishing their contact with the community – so he was advised to submit an application in the usual way for competitive tender.

The Home Office is one of the largest departments and it is one of the most varied in the responsibilities which it undertakes. It is also the Department that gets saddled with unknown matters which no other Department could reasonably claim. When anything goes wrong, or when anything is catastrophic it is ten to one that the

Home Office will then have a role in it. Take the police for example. We established the Police Complaints Authority on a different basis and we put Sir Cecil Clothier QC in charge as Chairman and provided a qualified team of people to enter into investigations on behalf of the public at large in matters affecting police behaviour. They were to examine cases against the police, or which the police were undertaking to determine whether it was being done properly. It was a third party influence which gradually came to establish a good reputation for assistance in matters which the police had perhaps mishandled in their own right. We also established coordination between the police services and the Metropolitan Police, particularly in the matter of drugs, including the setting up of the National Drugs Intelligence Unit for the pooling of resources in the tracing of drugs which of course involved a lot of forces between supplier and consumer. This quickly led to further discussions on an international level with countries that were involved in the drug supply chain worldwide. It was an area of policing which caused enormous problems because of the scale of resources it required.

In the arena of betting and gaming we improved conditions for betting shops which could now offer light refreshments and make their windows more attractive, and we looked closely at the possibility of privatising the Tote. This proved much more difficult than we expected as there was a considerable lack of knowledge of who actually owned the Tote. It was not a profit-making body in the normal use of that term because of course it ploughed its profits back in and distributed to its punters. It was clearly doing very well within the racing community and there were very few problems associated with its running. We therefore decided to leave it alone for the moment.

Going round gaming institutions at night was interesting but a bit alarming. Interesting because you saw a lot of activity going on in the casinos which were licensed to trade at that time of day, but slightly alarming when you saw in places like the Golden Nugget lots of Chinese pouring over the dice surrounded by fumes of smoke. They seemed to pile in from the Chinese takeaways and laundries at a given hour of the early morning and keep going until their shops reopened. As far as one could see it was a totally orderly arrangement and there was very little noise, merely very great concentration.

Department of Trade and Industry

After two years at the Home Office I was posted in 1986 to become Minister of State for Industry in the Department of Trade and Industry for what was as it turned out my final year in Government. I arrived to find the Civil Servants who worked in the automotive division which was the largest division over which I presided had very low morale. I believe this was largely due to the activities of my predecessor, Mr Peter Morrison, who frankly did not like Civil Servants, broadly distrusted them and referred to them quite blatantly as Martians, which was hardly a sobriquet of endearance. My first act, therefore, was to assemble as many members of the division as I could, to give them a short address as to my attitudes to the work in hand and my strong commitment and belief in the role of the Civil Service in making my task acceptable. I think this helped the spirit to rise a little, but we did have substantial problems.

One of the last of the nationalised industries over which we presided (and it has to be remembered that the DTI handled a great many nationalised industries as the operative arm of government) was that of shipbuilding. This had been in steady decline for years but was now showing signs of collapse. The order books were very thin and in many cases it was specialist ships which kept the work going as opposed to the warships which had not been replaced as the budget for the Royal Navy was so restrained. The European market was highly competitive and the Germans were much favoured in the building and repairing of ships in places like Bremerhaven and Hamburg. The Dutch, too, with their longstanding devotion to the sea were very keen competitors. We did our best to find orders and we did our best also to try and merge some shipbuilders with others to try and sustain a more profitable base. Certainly the yards on the Clyde were seriously reduced and the one at Govan was about the only one to survive in its original scale. Our major thrust was to try and find alternative work in these depressed areas to try and reduce the impact of the closure of yards. To some extent the industry was the beneficiary of the oil industry with its demands for rigs, many of which were built in specially selected parts of Scotland with deep access to the sea. But this was very much a specialist field and more akin to steel fabrication than to building ships. There was also the importance of nuclear submarines which had special applications in Barrow and in Birkenhead.

The other major industry in which I was engaged was the automotive industry and in particular the large nationalised undertaking known as British Leyland which was originally BMC, the British Motor Corporation. This was a large and ailing conglomerate which had never been able to reach the levels of profit that its investment required. We were fortunate to find a dynamic Canadian named Graham Day who was picked to run this enterprise; and we managed to merge British Leyland Trucks with a Dutch company, DAF which was a much more promising competitor in the European market. The construction of Leyland trucks still took place at Garstang and Leyland in Lancashire where they had a facility second to none. But the range of motor cars had to be restricted if we were to get reasonable profit from the motor group itself. Eventually it was decided to concentrate on the Rover products which had a very distinguished pedigree and which had in Land Rover one of the world's best 4 x 4 vehicles, with both military and civilian demand. Under Graham Day Rover was given extra focus and effort and it started to pay dividends. Ultimately Rover attracted the eye of British Aerospace and that's where it ended up, with Graham Day joining the Aerospace board.

The need to reinvigorate the Rover range, and in particular to find appropriate engines for the middle-sized car, took me to visit Honda in Japan and to seek to interest that company in a shareholding in Rover Group. This was not forthcoming but we did get agreements with Honda to supply their engines to the middle-sized Rover models with considerable marketing success as a result. Honda had already established an engine plant at Swindon and this was the source of Rover's new engines. This arrangement worked exceedingly well but sadly we couldn't persuade Honda to make a direct investment in the Rover company. My Secretary of State at the DTI

At home with Dione and Rufus, 1992.

was Paul Channon. He was a delightful person to work with and he managed to maintain the DTI after the Westland Helicopters furore leading to the resignation of the previous Secretary of State, Mr Leon Brittan.

When the election was called in 1987 I personally decided to bring my ministerial career to an end, believing that a diet of red boxes was not necessarily the most exciting food in life. I was also missing significant parts of my young family growing up – we had three children and my wife had to bear the whole load of the family. So I returned cheerfully to the back benches, becoming a member of the Speaker's Panel of Chairmen for Standing Committees, Treasurer of the 1922 Committee and latterly Chairman of the Select Committee on Science and Technology.

I enjoyed Westminster and the wide range of interesting people who are there on all sides of the House. If you scratched around you would probably find that I got on reasonably well with colleagues on the Government benches as well as on the Opposition side. You have got to have the capacity to build bridges and get on, as far as generalities will allow, with Members of different political persuasions. This is essential in select committee work.

I suppose you could say that I have never been overtly ambitious and this may be a weakness in a politician. I have been much more a team player, making my contribution to groups of people. With one career behind me my ambition was to make another one at Westminster and I feel very gratified that I was able to do so.

Epilogue

Entertaining the Adventurers

THE COMPANY OF York Merchant Adventurers is a guild that has been in existence for over six centuries and Giles spoke twice at their famous Venison Feast. The feast is held every year in the Great Hall in York, a unique wooden structure of national importance.

The Guild's history embraced most of the rich York traders, who came together in the fourteenth and fifteenth century to regulate commerce, including standards and training. Individual merchants risked (adventured) their own capital, but did so within a common framework of trading regulations. The merchants of York were probably the most important after those of London, and their trade reached Spain, France, Holland and Germany. This history of the Adventurers, with the approach to wealth creation coupled with their international outlook no doubt appealed to Giles as a good example of 'One Nation' Conservativism put into practice.

This speech is taken from the Venison Feast of 1998, and with the year 2000 approaching, Giles wondered how the 'Millennium Bug', the apparent scourge of the modern economy, could possibly make its presence felt among the Merchant Adventurers . . .

Merchant Adventurer Speech
Friday, 6 November 1998

I rise, Mr Governor, with great difficulty to address this toast so well proposed by that splendid Adventurer, Mr Trevor Copley.

The oldest among you here will probably recall the fact that this is the second time I have endeavoured to do this within nine years. Governor Wheway was in post at that time and now it is Governor Burgess. It is quite possible that the material is identical but I frankly haven't dared to check it out.

I had thought that I might be buoyed up in my endeavours by information coming pouring in from your guests to say how glad they were that I was going to speak on their behalf, giving me advice and counsel as to how I might best achieve it, bearing in mind that my reservoir of knowledge of their individual capacities is limited to put it mildly. Sadly, however, I have not been buoyed up by the scale of letters pouring in to my humble address and thus I have no real appreciation about what all your guests do and I have no constructive role to play based upon an intimate knowledge of their affairs. Indeed, my capacity to handle this toast is much the same as it was nine years ago. I have no business to be here, I have no knowledge to deploy on their collective or individual behalf and I find myself in the darkness of ignorance – which is so typical of a Minister of the Crown.

Ministers are frequently called out to do something at short notice on behalf of their Secretary of State who decides that the event in question is not worthy of his presence at a rather late date. I once had to do a speech to the 70th anniversary of the Concrete Association.

This riotous engagement proved too much for the Secretary of State for Trade and Industry, I certainly would have turned it down myself were it not for the fact that it occurred at the Savoy Hotel with a captive audience of about 300 plus. I was duly furnished with the Secretary of State's alarmingly long address on the merits of the Association and its wonderful achievements over 70 years of life. I found this particular compendium a matter *per ardua ad tedium.*

I, therefore, decided to break ranks and I made a few opening remarks to this substantial audience and invited them, on a show of hands, to say would they rather have me read to them the Secretary of State's inspiring address about their Association or would they like to hear a few of the things that actually do go on in Government but never actually appear in the public domain. We had therefore a small referendum. On a show of hands the Secretary of State lost, hands down! And as I had been foolhardy enough to make the offer I then lay the mighty address aside and set out on a totally unscripted, un-thought-out and totally spontaneous description of a day in the life of a Junior Minister.

At the conclusion of this I got a standing ovation and a panic telephone call from the Private Secretary to the Secretary of State demanding to know on what authority I had dealt with this matter when the Secretary of State's address had, of course, been circulated well in advance to the most important and most likely newspapers who were willing to print it. Now taking a similar risk on this occasion I am reasonably confident that nothing that I say will be of remote interest to anybody except those in this room and that we might get along famously together if the same course were to be pursued.

Looking round the assembly, Mr Governor, I have to note that we are all getting quite a bit older. I think that sales of Viagra amongst the Merchants will prove highly profitable. At least I am on safe ground in saying that all your guests would wish me to thank you most sincerely for the scale of your hospitality, the warmth of your comradeship here and the sheer splendour of holding this event in such an absolutely stunning environment as this great Hall.

I was very glad to receive from your retiring Clerk this admirable little note that he has prepared on the history of the Hall and the history of the Company. I noted in particular on page 2 the graphic description of the way in which the Hall was built between 1357-1361. When I read about the Upper Level I have to say I was just a little concerned about one element in the description.

'The Great Hall is framed in timbers of English oak which grew plentifully in the Vale of York. They are fitted together with scarf, lap and mortice-and-tenon joints secured with wooden pegs.'

I must say, on behalf of your guests, let me sound a tiny little warning of the humble peg. Many a good rustic made pegs for a living but whether they would survive 500 years of undisturbed strain I began to wonder. Now let's say at the outset that 1359 was an absolutely cracking year for pegs. Peg men of Easingwold and Helperby floundering their way through the Forest of Galtres by night, a glowing lantern in each hand in order to get to the best pegs before sundown, struck me as a perfectly feasible operation in terms of the volume of pegs collected from the great forests. They obviously were cut from the sapling oak which would be shooting from the roots of the giant oak trees in the forest. They would be cut down and chopped to size with every possibility of reaching the correct diameter of the holes in which they were to be banged. So I put it to you quite simply, I began to wonder whether all the pegs had filled all the space which had been allocated to them. In other words they were driven right through in order to make clear, beyond doubt, that there was no vacuum in which that intrepid little character the *aurora borealis quercus* could make his little nest. Because these chaps are very determined. They bored for Britain for centuries – 400 years is not a daunting gestation period. In fact the timing could well be perfect, that come the Millennium the real Millennium bug will turn out to be *aurora borealis quercus*. Possibly this could be the last great service rendered by Lord Ivison of Wheatley to accept the challenging appointment of Peg Master to tap his way into the record books of saving this ancient structure. No better man than he could be appointed Baron of The Hanseatic League for services to the Adventurers of York.

Turning now to your theme, Mr Governor, I have to say that I am not qualified to be a Mariner amongst the august representatives that we see here today. Mind you I could claim two weeks of carrying the temporary appointment of the First Lord of the Admiralty combined a slender qualification. One week I was treading the boards of Sedbergh School, the next the boards of the Folk Hall in New Earswick. The same opera, the same full houses, but alas the show immediately closed thereafter. Thus I stuck close to my desk and never went to sea, but I enjoyed two weeks as Ruler of the Queen's Navee!

As Conservative candidate for the West Hull seat which included St Andrew's fish dock within its limits I met my first trawlerman at my inaugural meeting when a chap at the back of the hall stood up after my stirring address and asked me the following question: 'I would like to ask the candidate's opinion of the Merchant Shipping Act of 1894.' I began by saying I had never heard of it but, I said, although I know very little about the Merchant Shipping Act of 1894 if it is as old as that it should be repealed. Quite right he said. He turned out to be the mate of a striking trawler in Hull dock, a lifelong member of the Labour Party. So that year I doubled the Labour majority in West Hull, single handed. And it has been a safe Labour haven ever since.

As far as Adventurers are concerned I always thought that Adventurers always sailed close to the wind and thus were mariners at heart. But they were also buccaneers. I met three of them in the course of my Ministerial career.

The first was Mr John Zachary de Lorean whose motorcar company was established in Belfast to sell an extremely expensive two seater tart trap to West Coast California. He was sailing extremely close to the wind with bank accounts in funny countries, with huge debts largely sustained by a generous Socialist government of which my contribution out of £89 million was a modest £17 million.

The second venturer I met was at the Department of Environment when I was put in charge of the London Development Corporation by Michael Heseltine. The Chairman he selected for this particular Board was Sir Nigel Broakes of Trafalgar House. His claim to be a Mariner rested in his acquisition of the Cunard Group in this period. We had wonderful discussions over lunch, usually served on gold plate at one or other of his London Club houses, either the Berkeley or the Ritz. I am happy to say that the London Docks Development Corporation long outlived him and was a major success in the redevelopment of derelict docklands.

The third buccaneer I met was at the Home Office when I was in charge of, amongst other things, broadcasting which included those days of issuing franchises for cable and allied companies. I had a call one morning at 10.30 from a veteran named Mr Robert Maxwell. We eventually found a chair large enough in the Home Office to allow Captain Bob to be seated. He stated his business, he wanted to buy a franchise, he wanted to buy it now, didn't want any other franchises and would I quickly sanction the deal and he wouldn't waste much time any further. I refused his entreaty and said I would make a note and let him know when the bidding would open, because they were all going to be put to competitive tender. I wished him a happy day and never saw him again. Indeed it was only a few days after this event that he decided to walk upon the water off the coast of Tenerife from the deck of his yacht Ghislaine and the rest is history.

We have amongst this company many who come from a distinguished line of seafarers, none perhaps more distinguished than that of P.V. Addyman. The V of course stands for Viking to whose contribution to York Peter Addyman has done more than anybody else to preserve. And in case it should be forgotten the name Viking ... bears the initial V. Every Viking longboat carried an Addyman whose task it was to count the oarsmen and to ensure that all the oars were properly manned all the time. He ticked off their names and numbers on the Addystick which he carried as his badge of office.

He tells me the tale of one of his ancestors who during his rounds of the ship discovered an oarsman slumped at his oars. It was No.23. When he asked why he had stopped rowing No. 23 looked at him with a baleful eye and said 'It's me 65th birthday and I'm retiring.' With this information Addyman went to the Captain of the ship.

'Captain, permission to speak. No. 23 has decided to stop rowing because he says it's his birthday and he has retired. What shall I do ?'

'Go back and throw No. 23 overboard, he's no further use to us and then give 20 lashes to each of the rest of the crew.

'Permission to speak.'

'OK Addyman what is it?'

'I fully understand throwing No. 23 overboard, why do I have to give 20 lashes to the rest of the crew?'

'You should know Addyman that it is a longstanding tradition that when anybody retires you always have a bit of a whip round amongst the lads.'

And thus was established a pattern of behaviour brought by the Vikings which we now of course regard as standard practice.

> An Englishman true is the Addyman
> He's always a good, not a Baddyman
> The Welshman sings gladly, he's a Gladdyman
> The Scotsman pipes sadly, he's a Saddyman
> But the Irishman – well he's just a Paddyman

Peter's Cambridge tutor discovered more about the Irish Paddyman and has supplied a little extra verse referring to the nefarious activities of these individuals.

> The Paddyman is coming – his foot is on the stair
> Abandon O abandon hope all ye who enter there
> The Paddyman is coming. I hear with mounting dread
> The echoing percussions of his greatly muffled tread
> The Paddyman is coming. He's over-run the Bailey
> The Motte resists him still though he tilts at it twice daily.

So we come to the final part. Whatever the future might hold, it does at least ensure that the honour, integrity and history of this great gathering of Merchants and Mariners will continue to have its place in the City of York. If it does continue to flourish then even the Paddyman may not pose much of a threat. I am just a touch less sanguine about our little dear friend *aurora borealis quercus* because since I have been speaking he has nudged a millimetre closer to the Millennium point.

On behalf of all your guests may I thank you in the appropriate manner by saying your welcome has been most cordial and your cordial has been most welcome.

Letter

Giles's handwriting was always notoriously difficult to read, and his degree from Cambridge was starred for illegibility. He always preferred to chat on the phone, when the need arose he wasn't averse to putting pen to paper for family letters. Here is a letter to Henrietta, who was at that time working in Hong Kong, and had typically remembered that July the 22nd 1987 was his investiture day. The day was helped along by Patricia Ellison, Giles's mother in law who at that time supervised the Crown Equerry's Household at the Royal Mews.

Dear Hen,

How very kind of you to remember that yesterday was investing day and how good of you to ring up. Herewith is a blow by blow account: Weather – menacing but not wet. As we bowled up to Buck House with car sticker to gain entry into the inner courtyard (n.b. we stopped at the Royal Mews en route to place 1 x Dom Perignon '76 reverently in the fridge!) I was sent one way, Mum, Tory and Chris another to take their seats on a dais in the State Ball Room. I was then weeded out from the recipients of lower orders and arrived in an outer room with the other knights – twenty in all! A much larger crop than usual because of four MPs – R. Boyson, G. Pattie, me and the new Solicitor General (Nicholas Lyell Q.C.). The General in charge of ceremonies duly arrived to teach us the form – including the 'Kneeler' for practice! Several of the lads were elderly, including a charming old constitutional lawyer from Mauritius! We then formed a crocodile in alphabetical order and I was tail end Charlie! Douglas Hurd, as Home Secretary, read out the list of Knights Batchelor and before you could say Queen Elizabeth II, I was marching across the ballroom, turning sharp left, bowing, three more steps, kneeling (unlike others my right leg left the ground!) Then one tap on each shoulder with the *flat* blade of the sword. I stood up and took two steps forward and she placed a big yellow and gold riband over my neck with a gold badge dangling therefrom. We had a little chat: 'How long an MP. . . ? How long a Minister? How kind of you to come!! And we shook hands and parted the best of friends! Frogmarched to the back of the 'all and sat down with me mates.

All told, the investiture – including two recipients of the Polar Medal and one Ghurkha major – lasted one and a quarter hours. Lots of people, lots of finery and guardsmen, Yeomen and band playing softly. Then after photographs (at vast prices) we joined up with Grannie, Will and Liz who had filtered into the courtyard (!) and we swept off to lunch taking the Patties (including Andrew) to the Mews. 2 x D Perignon (76 and a '71 that Grannie had 'acquired'!!) 2 x Mumm and 3 x Sancerre with the caviar, the salmon and the strawberries, followed by pineapple pavlova and coffee en tout. A monumental meal! We rose at 3.15!! What a day.

Today we went back for the Garden Party – just like old times to see QE II again! We raised many a glass to absent friends (I think!).

Lots of love from us all.

Dad.

Speech to Pudsey Constituency Annual/Farewell Dinner on Friday, 28 November 1997

As we look back over this last year I suggest we should not do so in anger. The Conservatives suffered a very substantial disaster and the loss of the Pudsey constituency was but a small part of it. I suggest there should be no recriminations against the candidate, the organisation, the agent, the previous MP or the members themselves. What took place was a shifting of the tectonic plates on the body politic. The shift was a deliberate choice by the electorate which I suspect would have occurred whatever the policies John Major's government sought to pursue, whatever the state of unity in his party or whoever was leading the party. I frankly doubt if sleaze in whatever form had been totally absent that the result would have been significantly different. But the reason why we lost is perversely the reason why we won in 1992. Then Labour was found at the very last minute to be unelectable. Kinnock was shown to be all pith and wind and not of Prime Ministerial quality. A triumphalist rally in Sheffield showed that Old Labour was alive and kicking.

Subsequently after John Smith's early breakthrough Tony Blair, public school and Oxford educated, showed incredible energy and vigour and not a little courage in conducting major surgery on the Labour Party to rid it of many of its fetid organs: out went the old Labour Party constitution, out went Trade Union domination, in came capitalist policies of economic management, out went nationalisation, nuclear disarmament, public expenditure increases and high taxation. In came constitutional reform, devolution, tight control of public spending, central vetting of candidates, marginal-ising of the party conference and broader and deeper cooperation with the EEC. It was not long before the opinion polls started to show that Labour electability was rising fast. If we add to that the strongest argument against us, namely, Time for a Change, Labour frankly were unstoppable. To be sure disunity in the Government, outbreaks of sleaze and the collapse of our cohesion were clear signs that the Conservatives were running out of steam and the Conservative Government itself was rapidly losing its majority and with it its credibility. So let's be clear, we won in 1992 exceptionally and against the odds. Labour won in 1997 predictably and with the odds.

So what do we do now? I think we are bound to recognise that it will be a long haul back. It will not only take a long time but such is the scale of our defeat that we need to comprehensively reform, renew and replace our policies and to make them relevant not for today but for a decade hence.

We start at least with one great advantage: which is that Conservatism is a pragmatic philosophy, it is not written down in tablets of stone. At its core is the capitalist system of economics operating through the private sector which is free of state intervention but for which the state must provide stable economic conditions and access to free markets. I trust that working parties and groups based on the Conservative Research Department are already engaged in working out predictably different and new policies from New Labour suitable for the electorate in 2000 and beyond.

Second we must radically reform and rebuild the structure of the party. I fully support the changes being made already in the wake of the new Leadership's initiative. With regard to the election of the Party Leader, that, too, must be reformed, but we must remember that the existing system provides for the parliamentary party to trigger a leadership contest if the leader, be it in government or in opposition fails to carry a significant majority of the parliamentary party with him or her. I seem to recall that in the most recent leadership election the National Union's poll of constituencies was firmly in favour of Kenneth Clarke. I am bound to say that if I had been involved in that election I would have endorsed that view. But it does show the width of the gap between MPs and Members of the Party in the country which on future occasions must surely be narrowed not only by consultation but by direct participation in the voting as well.

The election of William Hague as Leader was a dramatically high risk for the party to take. But his generation is his greatest asset and with almost five years as Leader ahead of him before the next election he has plenty of opportunity to gain both in stature and experience before his first major test arrives. I have no doubt that the media will see to it that he gets a bumpy ride for much of the time. But his first few months in office have demonstrated a sharp mind and a quick intelligence which bodes well for the future. I have to say I have not been happy with the way he has handled the European Monetary issue. We went through many anguishing phases in the last parliament before a form of words was designed which would broadly hold the parliamentary party together. Now I am well aware that many of my good friends on the liberal wing of the Conservative Party (pause for groans) have lost their seats or in the case of Temple-Morris lost their marbles and insofar as many of Mrs Thatcher's children were standing at this election the balance of the new parliamentary party has shifted towards the Euro-sceptic wing. But for the life of me I don't see the need for the Conservative attitude to the European issue being widened and hardened in this way. Opposition politics is hardly a political activity which demands a 10-year view on anything. But on this issue it is more than likely that it will be settled by those in Government and not in Opposition, especially with a Government majority of 140 plus.

What I am fearful of is that William Hague will be caught in the same vortex as J Major whereby he will be pushed to take the policy stance even further and broadening the anti-Europe attitude to include other aspects of Community policy. This could fatally undermine our present economic buoyancy and make it more difficult for overseas investors to develop their plants and European access from within the UK. Having lost two able members of his Front Bench team and aroused the antagonism of the two most senior ministers from the previous government, this has caused a problem which I am sure the media will keep fanning for all they are worth. I don't think that was either necessary or wise.

The Leader, quite rightly wishes to focus the Party in a stance on the matter which will carry public support. If we are to be populist then it seems to me necessary to flesh out the reasons or the conditions under which we continue to maintain this stance as an ongoing political commitment. In my view the likely scenario is that the Labour Government will probably take its formal decision prior to the next election and could well hold the referendum that it has promised at the same time as the General Election in say 2002. If the Labour Government is re-elected and if the referendum is positive then the issue will frankly disappear.

My anxiety also is that Opposition politics is about flexibility. It is about taking pragmatic decisions as the issues arise, primarily for the discomfiture of the existing administration. In our search for a refashioning of appeal for the Conservative cause our requirement is to set out our long-term objectives firmly and to provide the case for a new Conservative Government with a wider appeal than hitherto and with some new and developable policies suitable for a new style of government. By the time of the next election it looks as though there *will* be Scottish and Welsh devolution. It seems more than likely there will be some regional assemblies. It seems pretty certain that London will get an elected Mayor and possibly an elected assembly. It also seems certain that both for the European elections in 1999 and for the election to regional assemblies or for the Scottish Parliament that some form of proportional representation will be introduced. The LibDem alliance will settle for nothing less. This may well transform single member constituencies. This series of changes in our national fabric will accomplish a major devolvement of central government. It will be populist and . . . of Blair's determinations to establish New Labour as the People's Party under the People's PM in Presidential mode. After the tragedy of the People's Princess we have seen the evolution of the People's Monarchy last week fashioned by Blair. This is very clever stuff.

I for one would like to see the Conservative Party devising a new policy of support for local government *as it is*. For far too long within the last 18 years our party has sought to control or reduce the power and influence of local government as well as to restrict substantially the share of its expenditure. If we want to rebuild this party then I believe it is within each local constituency and within each ward within our association that we should start to rebuild it. For far too long we have tended to ignore the importance of local government and the value of those who serve within it. Yet we all know that the reason why local associations like ours exist is to maintain a local Conservative presence in the local authorities. Politics in our communities starts with council elections and successful local elections nearly always lead to successful national elections. Bearing in mind that elections occur nearly every year and bearing in mind that the unpopularity of the national government is a major factor in determining how people vote in local elections we should pursue a new initiative specially designed to restore decision making to the most local level wherever possible. It is not regional tiers for local administration that we want nor indeed provincial parliaments. What we need is more effective policies which provide for Conservatives and Conservative Councillors to demonstrate that we support government at the most local level. We should fashion policies which will encourage it to have budgets to spend on what local people really want in their communities. The best possible relationship we can build up with electors is one where they can see the benefit of what they vote for as near to their homes as possible.

Finally a word about national institutions. There is no doubt that our institutions are in decline. People's respect of the law is to put it mildly questionable and the public appetite for committing crime seems inexhaustible. The influence of the churches in respect of moral leadership and public acceptance seems weaker than ever. Respect for the monarchy has clearly declined though not nearly as fast or as far as the lack of respect for Members of Parliament or indeed for Parliament itself. These are issues which the Conservative Party, always traditional in its values, must defend.

So as we Conservatives begin our long road to renaissance for the Conservative Party we must not look back in anger or despair but we must look forward not just in hope but in genuine expectation. We have the time and I believe we have the talents. In our leader we have a young man of outstanding talent who has yet to develop it to the full. He must be given the time and space to do so. After the previous debacle in 1945 there was a massive flowering of Tory talent, Macleod, Butler, Heath, Keith Joseph, yes, and Enoch Powell who provided the philosophical powerhouse around which new Conservative policies and aims were fashioned. Out of this 'One Nation politics' was born and became the means by which we gradually re-established ourselves as a cohesive force in post-war Britain. In education and in housing and in health and in economic management, in trade union reform, privatisation, in the selling of council houses, in the free flow of capital both in and out of the UK all these provided an anti-Socialist impact which was both constructive and liberalising in its effect. No wonder that for 18 years our party was trusted as the one solid bulwark against Socialist excess. That legacy has now been inherited by a party which has shed Socialism itself. We are, therefore, in some way, the victims of our own success. But our arrogance clearly outstripped the level of public acceptance which we had come to rely upon. Now there is a time for renewal of confidence but laced with humility, for renewal of policies and philosophies which run *with* the grain of public feeling and not against it. We must be simple and not obscure, generous and not mean, united by a real conviction and a new sense of purpose and not dragooned piecemeal by fear and threat. It can be done, it must be done, I'm sure it will be done.

After nearly 25 years in representing the Conservative cause in Pudsey I thank you all for allowing me the honour and privilege of being your MP. Dione and I thank you for the generosity of your spirit and for the warmth of your friendship and for the steadfast loyalty you have shown in good times and in bad. A Happy Christmas and may the New Year be better than the last. Let me conclude with Dickens: '"God Bless us everyone," said Tiny Tim, "I'll be last of all".'

Index

Page numbers in italics denote illustrations